MW01156538

"If you're looking for ways to infuse new
or a lifeline to get started, *Welcome to*
Stacey and Lynne share practical, qu.
the research-based writing process work in your classroom.

—JEFF ANDERSON, AUTHOR OF *PATTERNS OF POWER: INVITING YOUNG WRITERS
INTO THE CONVENTIONS OF LANGUAGE, GRADES 1–5*

"Chocked to the brim with the day-to-day advice that teachers want and need,
*Welcome to Writing Workshop* is an instant classic."

—RUTH CULHAM, AUTHOR OF *TEACH WRITING WELL*

"After reading *Welcome to Writing Workshop*, you'll have the knowledge and practical
ideas you need to inspire EVERY writer in your classroom."

—MARIA WALTHER, FIRST-GRADE TEACHER AND INSTRUCTIONAL SPECIALIST,
INDIAN PRAIRIE DISTRICT 204, AURORA, IL
AND AUTHOR OF *THE RAMPED-UP READ ALOUD*

"If you are looking for the behind-the-scenes work that goes into a writing
workshop, *Welcome to Writing Workshop* will be your go-to resource. It will be your
mentor text as you plan instruction and develop systems and structures
to bring writing workshop to life in your classroom."

—CLARE LANDRIGAN & TAMMY MULLIGAN,
AUTHORS OF *IT'S ALL ABOUT THE BOOKS*

"With a pronounced reverence for teachers, for students, and for the literacy giants
whose shoulders we all stand on, Stacey and Lynne offer us a bright,
undiluted vision for what writing workshop can (and should) be."

—SHAWNA COPPOLA,
AUTHOR OF *RENEW! BECOME A BETTER—AND MORE AUTHENTIC—WRITING TEACHER*

"Stacey and Lynne's book is like having your own personal
literacy coach at your fingertips. I've had many teachers request
a professional book like this, and now it's here."

—PAULA BOURQUE, AUTHOR OF *CLOSE WRITING* AND *SPARK!
QUICK WRITES TO KINDLE HEARTS AND MINDS IN ELEMENTARY CLASSROOMS*

"In *Welcome to Writing Workshop*, Stacey Shubitz and Lynne Dorfman do exactly for teachers what we strive to do for our student writers: meet them where they are and help them take those next steps to be successful at their craft."

—KAREN BIGGS-TUCKER,
AUTHOR OF *TRANSFORMING LITERACY TEACHING IN THE ERA OF HIGHER STANDARDS: GRADES 3–5*

"With passion and expertise, Stacey and Lynne have thought of everything from the big ideas to the small details to ensure writing workshop is joyful, purposeful, and meaningful for students."

—KATIE EGAN CUNNINGHAM,
AUTHOR OF *STORY: STILL THE HEART OF LITERACY LEARNING*

"*Welcome to Writing Workshop* is a guide full of important information for new and veteran teachers. Stacey and Lynne bring together the latest research in teaching writing and putting students at the center of their learning."

—DR. LORRAINE DEROSA,
ELEMENTARY SUPERVISOR OF LITERACY
LOWER MERION SCHOOL DISTRICT

"*Welcome to Writing Workshop* gets right to the point: teaching writing through the workshop model IS necessary and possible in every classroom."

—DR. AILEEN HOWER,
GRADUATE PROGRAM COORDINATOR FOR THE M.ED. IN LANGUAGE AND LITERACY
AND ASSISTANT PROFESSOR OF LITERACY AT MILLERSVILLE UNIVERSITY

"With clarity and conviction, Stacey and Lynne remind us of what is possible when we remember that students—not testing, standards, or mandates— should be at the heart and soul of our teaching."

—DR. GRACE ENRIQUEZ,
ASSOCIATE PROFESSOR, LANGUAGE & LITERACY DIVISION,
LESLEY UNIVERSITY AND DEPARTMENT EDITOR,
CHILDREN'S LITERATURE REVIEWS, LANGUAGE ARTS

*Welcome to*

# WRITING WORKSHOP

# Welcome to

# WRITING
# WORKSHOP

## ENGAGING TODAY'S STUDENTS
## WITH A MODEL THAT WORKS

**STACEY SHUBITZ & LYNNE R. DORFMAN**

*Foreword by Kate Roberts and Maggie Beattie Roberts*

**Stenhouse Publishers**

**Portsmouth, New Hampshire**

# Stenhouse
## PUBLISHERS
www.stenhouse.com

Video footage provided by Ralph Abbott.

Videos

Big Red Kangaroo. Text copyright © 2013 by Claire Saxby. Illustrations copyright © 2013 by Graham Byrne. Reproduced by permission of the publisher, Candlewick Press, Somerville, MA on behalf of Walker Books, Australia.

p. 3 Figure 1.2 From *The Construction Zone* by Terry Thompson, copyright © 2015, reproduced with permission of Stenhouse Publishers. www.stenhouse.com.

p. 107 Figure 7.5 Adapted from *Micro Lessons in Writing* by Jim Vopat. Copyright © 2007 by James Vopat. Published by Heinemann, Portsmouth, NH. Reprinted by permission of Publisher. All Rights Reserved.

Library of Congress Cataloging-in-Publication Data

Names: Shubitz, Stacey, 1977—author. | Dorfman, Lynne R., 1952—author.
Title: Welcome to writing workshop : engaging today's students with a model that works / Stacey Shubitz and Lynne R. Dorfman.
Description: Portsmouth, New Hampshire : Stenhouse Publishers, [2019] | Includes bibliographical references.
Identifiers: LCCN 2018046513 (print) | LCCN 2018059926 (ebook) | ISBN 9781625311672 (ebook) | ISBN 9781625311665 (pbk. : alk. paper)
Subjects: LCSH: English language—Composition and exercises—Study and teaching (Elementary) | English language—Rhetoric—Study and teaching (Elementary) | Creative writing (Elementary education)
Classification: LCC LB1576 (ebook) | LCC LB1576 .S41455 2019 (print) | DDC 372.6—dc23
LC record available at https://lccn.loc.gov/2018046513

Cover design, interior design, and typesetting by Gina Poirier, Gina Poirier Design

Manufactured in the United States of America

PRINTED ON 30% PCW
RECYCLED PAPER
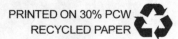

25 24 23 22 21 20          9 8 7 6 5 4 3 2

## FROM STACEY

*For Marcia and Gerald Shubitz, who value education and lifelong learning. I feel fortunate—every single day— that you are my parents.*

## FROM LYNNE

*To friend and colleague Frank Murphy, a teacher of writers who writes! Thank you for supporting my efforts to continue writing professional books and, every so often, nudging me to try other writing formats, too.*

# Contents

# *Welcome to Writing Workshop Videos*

The videos are an integral part of our book that appear on our online companion website sten.pub/WritingWorkshop. As you read the chapters, you will find video icons we hope you will use to watch teachers and students engaged in the work of writing workshop. Below is a list of videos with a brief description that should be watched in conjunction with the explanations we provide within the chapters. Watch the videos when you need to think again about an important concept or routine. They are there to support you and cheer you on! We hope the videos, together with our discussions in the text, welcome you to a model that works—writing workshop—where everyone's a writer.

http://sten.pub/
WritingWorkshop

## AFTERWORD

# Foreword

In the childhood story *The Velveteen Rabbit* by Margery Williams Bianco, the Rabbit, new to the nursery, sits at the feet of the Skin Horse, a longtime companion and friend of the young boy. With a strong desire to make sense of his new world and role, the Rabbit seeks the advice of a wise mentor—a toy with experience, wisdom, and insight. The Rabbit asks, "What is REAL?" The Skin Horse ponders for a moment and responds, "It's a thing that happens to you."

"You become."

We had similar moments on our road to becoming teachers—moments when our younger selves sought the advice of more experienced colleagues; moments when our mentors saw promise in our youth. For Kate, it was in college. She wrote a personal essay for the first time, and when she read it aloud, her professor looked her straight in the eye and said, "You are a writer." And thus, she became one. The combination of a mentor's confidence and a hidden desire to become a writer created a spark that helped shape Kate's newly formed identity as writer. For Maggie, it was in high school. She sat in her guidance counselor's office, seeking advice of her major in college. After listening to Maggie talk about wanting to help children as a therapist, her counselor slid a pamphlet for a teaching scholarship across the table and said, "Have you ever thought about teaching?" The rest, as they say, is history.

You probably have a story like this—a time someone named a part of your dormant and undiscovered talent into being, awakening your calling to become a teacher.

This book is that calling. This book is the Skin Horse looking at all of us, calling us to become the real writing teacher we want to be.

Stacey and Lynne have managed to achieve the almost impossible: they have written a book that speaks to the highest goals we can have as writing teachers, while holding our hands every step of the way, helping us make it happen. We need this book. We needed it a long time ago, and we need it now. We, meaning our profession, but also "us," the authors of this foreword.

We needed this book when we began teaching. Back then, we were flailing around, trying new things, aware of the goals of writing workshop but less clear on how to make those goals a reality for our students. It was all trial and error and, oh goodness, so much error.

For any new teacher entering the teaching of writing, this book is the course you will need to provide students with empathic, powerful, productive, dreamy teaching. In it, you will be introduced to the basics of writing workshop, the goals and beliefs of writing workshop teachers, all while centering students by listening to their hopes and dreams. Stacey and Lynne write passionately and knowledgeably about these beliefs—they have lived them, they know they work, and they know you can do it.

Paired with their beliefs about the teaching of writing, Stacey and Lynne use their years of experience and craft a vision of writing workshop that is a sustainable, productive space for kids and teachers. You will find page after page of practical advice for how to manage twenty or more students' individual writing goals. Or how to consider what to teach your students and how to be as responsive as possible. Or how to give feedback to students that can nudge them in new directions in their writing. Or how to take students through a writing process so that each is able to go at their own pace, yet still be pushed in new directions by their writing partners, themselves, and you.

These are no small feats, but under the care of these authors, you feel you can do it. Stacey and Lynne are like the older sisters who take you under their wings and help you get ready for the big dance. They know what you need before you do, and by the end of your time with them, you are transformed, and so are your kids. If you are new to workshop, this book will help guide you with love, high ideals, and clear instructions for how to make it all work.

Of course, we are not new to workshop, and perhaps, neither are you. Perhaps, like us, you have been teaching writing workshop for a while, or your district has a writing workshop–based curriculum. At first, when we began this book, we felt like veterans. "Oh, we will probably know the stuff in here," we thought. We knew how to write a minilesson (though Stacey and Lynne's explanation is so clear and practical that we can't wait to share their take with teachers). We knew a bit about paper choice and materials (though their explanations for how to create systems for kid-centered choice feel fresh). We did, in fact, "know" some of the stuff in here.

Yet this book feels revolutionary to us. Not because it taught us what writing workshop is, but because it reminded us of what writing workshop used to be.

These days, writing workshop in many schools serves the standards and expectations of the district, the system, and even the tests that kids experience. While choice over what to write is present, there's not much time to nurture that choice, or, worse yet, the choice has been taken away—the choice of genre, purpose, or even audience does not exist as it once did. While there is independent writing, often there is such an abundance of work to be done just to get through the unit that kids don't have much time to wander, explore, or create. In some ways—big and small—writing workshop has morphed into an overly standardized, teacher-centered shell of what it used to be.

This book reminds us of what the promise of writing workshop was and can still be. Writing workshop can put children first—their interests, their knowledge, their creativity, pacing, and needs. As we read this book, we were reminded of our writing workshops of old. Workshops were places where kids could invent, create, engage, and discuss their writing with great freedom and support. They were places where students' voices were heard, cherished, and nurtured. They were places that we studied genres together and walked alongside great writing teachers in the pages of mentor texts. Writers wandered through the process, talking with one another, celebrating progress. You know, like real writers do.

Because that was the promise of writing workshop—that we should treat our students like real writers in the world. What Donald Murray, Lucy Calkins, Don Graves and others did was to show us the power of sitting down with a child, listening to their ideas, and helping their writing come alive. Not to make sure that all of our kids reach all the standards that have been put upon them by outside forces.

The promise of writing workshop is that if we help every child become a writer, they will write and think well. This book shows us ways we can thread that needle—how we can reach for high standards yet not at the expense of the heart and soul of our classrooms.

In many ways, we wish we could go back in time with this book in our hands. As new teachers, we would have been so much *better* with the advice we find in these pages. And yet we are also so glad that we have this book now—to reset our focus on our North Stars, to remember what is true and precious about a classroom full of young writers—their energy and creativity and abilities to write their own world into being.

—*Kate & Maggie*

# Acknowledgments

We are grateful for the many opportunities we have had to learn from teachers, students, administrators, and conference presenters across the country. Friends, family members, and colleagues have been our cheerleaders, encouraging our work on this project. When we came together more than three years ago to discuss the idea for a new book, we enthusiastically agreed on our title, *Welcome to Writing Workshop*, and embarked on a journey to help teachers everywhere imagine a writing workshop and embrace the idea of being a teacher of writers who writes.

We would like to extend our sincere thanks to the teachers whose classrooms are featured in this book: Katie Bristol, Kathryn Cazes, Kelsey Corter, Laura Deutsch, Deborah Driscoll, Diana Erben, Rachel Federbush, Shelly Keller, Amy Lynch, Cary S. Harrod, Suzanne Meyer, Molly Murray, and Kathleen Neagle Sokolowski. Your students are fortunate to work in such beautiful, kid-friendly spaces.

Melanie Meehan, thank you for organizing a full schedule to view writing workshop in action and interview teachers, administrators, and students from Tootin' Hills Elementary School in Simsbury School District. Thanks to classroom teachers Missie Champagne, Lisa Jacobs, and Lesley Turner for permitting us to videotape your writing workshops and interview you, too. Maggie Seidel, thank you for welcoming us to your school and allowing us to interview you about writing workshop. Betsy Gunsalus, Director of Curriculum in Simsbury, thank you for answering all our questions. Melanie, you were not only the tour guide, but led small groups, conferred with students, and modeled for us what a literacy coach can do to support teachers and writing workshop.

From Upper Moreland Primary School, we would like to thank teachers Kolleen Bell and Kelly Gallagher for their contributions of a kindergarten conference and second-grade status of the class session, respectfully.

Karen Rhoads, thank you for welcoming us into your fourth-grade classroom and letting us watch you and your students at work in writing workshop. Valerie Hawkins, thank you for time spent in your fifth-grade classroom. Upper Moreland School District has always been a welcoming place to learn from teachers and students and share that learning with teachers everywhere. Principals Dr. Michael Bair and Ms. Susan Smith, you have always been generous with your time and acted as cheerleaders for writing workshop. Superintendent of Schools, Dr. Robert Milrod, your encouragement and support has been unwavering! Thank you!

From Boyertown Area School District, a big thank-you to our friend and teacher extraordinaire Catherine Gehman and her wonderful fourth-grade writers who are featured on the cover of this book. Dr. Sara E. Obarow, Director of Professional Learning, Dr. Melissa Woodard, Assistant Superintendent, academics, and David P. Krem, acting superintendent, thank you for your support. Stephanie Landis, principal of Gilbertsville Elementary School, thank you for welcoming us to your school and taking time out of your busy schedule to speak with us. To Melissa Schmitz, instructional coach, we extend our gratitude for the support that enabled us to videotape the classroom and individual students and for your thoughtful responses to interview questions. We loved spending time with all of you!

Thanks to Frank Murphy and his sixth graders at Holland Elementary School in the Council Rock School District. It was amazing to observe the conferences and watch these writers in action. We would also like to extend our thanks to Dr. Robert Fraser, superintendent of schools, and Joseph MacClay, principal of Holland Elementary School. Dr. Susan Elliott, assistant superintendent for teaching and learning as well as our dear friend and colleague, thank you for welcoming us to Council Rock. We are thrilled to have Frank's class represent your district in this professional book on writing workshop.

A sincere thank-you to Ralph Abbott, who shot and edited all the videos that appear in this book. We appreciate your dedication to this project. Our book comes alive, thanks to all the video clips you recorded for us.

We have grown as teachers of writing thanks to the inspiring work of Lucy Calkins and her colleagues at the Teachers College Reading and

Writing Project. If you don't already have them, pick up the *Units of Study—Writing*, a valuable resource and teaching tool that will help you grow as a teacher of writers.

We have been fortunate to have our dear friend and editor William Varner with us throughout this journey. Bill, your support means everything to us. Thank you for answering all our questions and always believing in us. You helped us grow as writers and imagine the possibilities for this book. Thanks to everyone in the Stenhouse family, including Dan Tobin, Jay Kilburn, Stephanie Levy, Amanda Bondi, Lynne Costa, Shannon St. Peter, Nate Butler, Faye LaCasse, and Jill Backman, who have in various ways offered support and mentorship.

## From Stacey

In 2010, I dedicated *Day by Day: Refining Writing Workshop Through 180 Days of Reflective Practice* in memory of my first-grade teacher, Carol Snook, who encouraged me to write. A few years ago, I received a consulting request from a school close to where I grew up. During my conversation with the school's curriculum director, she revealed that she had noticed the *Day by Day* dedication to Carol, with whom she had taught in the 1980s. "You know Carol used the workshop model to teach writing, right?" this curriculum director said. I was stunned into silence—and then tears. Suddenly, everything fell into place. Carol called us writers. She encouraged us to write about a variety of topics. She featured our published books in the classroom library next to the bound books. It was clear to me that my incredible first-grade teacher was ahead of her time! I am thankful to Carol, since she planted a seed that blossomed into a writer. I cannot imagine a life in which I am not writing.

To my dear friend, colleague, and mentor, Lynne Dorfman: I recall the day we met for breakfast in Lancaster, and you approached me about coauthoring this book. Thank you for your willingness to wait until Ari was a few months old to begin. I'm thankful you became part of Isabelle's and Ari's lives while we were writing this book. (I think it helped Isabelle, especially, to get to know you so she wasn't resentful of all the times

"Mommy was working on the book.") What an enjoyable journey this has been!

I am inspired by my colleagues—who are brilliant educators—at *Two Writing Teachers*. Thank you, Lanny Ball, Kelsey Corter, Deb Frazier, Betsy Hubbard, Melanie Meehan, Beth Moore, and Kathleen Neagle Sokolowski for collaborating on TWT, and, most important, for your dedication to teaching young writers.

I have deep gratitude to the Slice of Life community, which gathers on Tuesdays year-round and every March at *Two Writing Teachers*. I am inspired by your stories and am fueled by your comments. Thank you for helping me grow as a writer.

Many thanks to Anna Gratz Cockerille, Grace Enriquez, Michelle Haseltine, Laurie Higgins, and Mary Howard for your willingness to answer my literacy questions. You always help me grow as an educator.

Thank you to my former students—at P.S. 171 and at The Learning Community—for teaching me how to teach writers.

Speaking of P.S. 171, I will always be grateful to my former principal, Dimitres Pantelidis, who provided me with the resources to launch and sustain writing workshop. In addition, he gave me the gift of time, so I could attend professional development to help me learn as much as I could about the teaching of writing during my first years in the classroom. In addition, Pat Werner, who was my literacy coach during my first year of teaching at P.S. 171, spent many hours chatting with me after school helping me to understand how to engage my students with a writing workshop. While the miles between us have kept us apart for years, I will always be thankful for Pat's wisdom and friendship.

Two of my cousins, Scott Shubitz and Jared Peet, and their spouses, Tiffany Hensley and Annie Infantino, are dedicated educators. I am grateful to have all of you to call upon personally and professionally.

My mother-in-law, Linda Schaefer, is a retired literacy coach and classroom teacher. However, she remains one of my go-to people when I need a sounding board about literacy. Thank you, Linda, for your continued willingness to "talk shop" with me even though you now spend your days as a devoted grandmother my children adore!

My children, Isabelle and Ari, light up my life. It is my hope you will come to see yourselves as writers, no matter what path you take in life.

My parents, Marcia and Gerald Shubitz, are among the finest parents out there. They encourage me professionally, share advice, and offer moral support when I need it. I am beyond grateful for their willingness to spend time with my children, especially when I'm working out of town or need time to write. Thank you for playing an integral part in Isabelle's and Ari's lives as "Bubbe and Zayde."

Writing this book wouldn't have been possible without the care and support of my husband, Marc Schaefer. Anytime I needed additional time to write, Marc entertained the kids at home or took them out so I could have a quiet house in which to write. I am thankful for your love and for your friendship. I could not ask for more.

## From Lynne

I am grateful to all my colleagues, especially my previous coauthors and dear friends, Rose Cappelli and Diane Dougherty. You have taught me a lot about organization and have helped me learn about the importance of planning and managing time. You are always there to listen, suggest, and encourage. I know I can count on you both. Thank you! Brenda Krupp, Karen Rhoads, Teresa Lombardi, Reene Martin, Teresa Moslak, Sue Powidzki, and Kathy Randolph, I must include you here, too. Your friendship means so much to me! Working in both your writing classrooms or working with you on presentations and graduate courses always inspired me. We had fun, too. Learning can be joyful!

I must always thank the Pennsylvania Writing & Literature Project and all my friends there—especially our past director, Dr. Mary Buckelew, and our current director, Dr. Pauline Schmidt. Being part of the PAWLP leadership team has helped me grow in many ways. My participation in the invitational summer writing institute in 1989 was the spark that fueled my passion to write professional books for teachers. I am proud to be a PAWLP fellow and NWP fellow. Mary, you have said many times that we have only one dance on this glorious planet, so we should make every day count and fill it with joy. That joy often comes from being with the people we love. Little moments like birthday celebrations at Nectar make writing days easier and more productive!

To PAWLP friends, Nancy McElwee, Janice Ewing, Rita Sorrentino, Patricia Smith, Tricia Ebarvia, Dana Kramaroff, Matthew Bloome, Jen Greene, Brian Kelley, Kelly Virgin, Brenda Krupp, Judy Jester, Patty Koller, Chris Kehan, Diane Quinn, Reene Martin, Teresa Moslak, Rita DiCarne, Sharon Williams, Warren Kulp, Peter Suanlarm, and Frank Murphy—you are dear colleagues who offer support, great advice, and the gift of friendship. Patti and Phil Sollenberger, you have been there since before the first *Mentor Texts*. How can I ever thank you for introducing Rose and me to our editor, Bill Varner! To my KSLA friends, Michael Williams, Ginny Williams, Frani Thomas, Jan Pizarro, Linda Horner, Pam Brandon, Anna Landers, Jane Helman, Hollie D'Agata, and Aileen Hower: you have always cheered me on!

I must thank the Upper Moreland School District where I was employed for thirty-eight years, its teachers, administrators, and students who supported and enriched my work as a writing coach and literacy coach. I am always there in spirit. During my time there, I grew as a writer, a teacher of writers, a team player, a literacy leader, a staff developer, and a reflective educator. Each year was new and rewarding.

To Stacey Shubitz, my coauthor and dear friend, I give my heartfelt thanks for your dedication and hard work, your attention to detail, and your willingness to collaborate on a book I have always wanted to write. Our "Unworkshop" days at Highlights Foundations, lunch dates in Lancaster, Skyping and phone conferences, and video-editing days with Ralph at your home have all made this project worthwhile and satisfying.

To my wonderful goddaughters, Alex, Brooke, and Cait, and their wonderful spouses, Steve, T.J., and Kevin, thank you for all the joy and love you give to me, filling me with renewed strength to work harder and smarter! The time we spend together is always precious time.

Thanks to my sister and brother-in-law, Diane and Willie, for being there for me and sharing my vacation away from writing time in Maine (although I finished final edits to send to Bill in August in a Portland hotel room while my husband was waiting for me at the checkout desk!).

A big thank-you to my wonderful husband, Ralph Abbott, who supported us by taking videos of classrooms and doing some video editing as well. You never once said you couldn't make the time for trips to Connecticut, Boyertown, or Council Rock for filming. I know you spent many evenings, long past midnight, watching and editing videos after already spending long hours watching them with Stacey and me while taking copious notes on what to trim and what to keep. I don't deserve you, but I am so glad you said, "I do!" five years ago. I simply cannot imagine a life without you by my side.

# Welcome, Teachers of Writers

I enter the room and immediately am impressed with the scratch-scratch sound of writing instruments moving across pages. Here, there seems to be choice. The youngsters, probably varying in age, use pencils of all sizes sharpened to a point, many of them with "No. 2" printed on the side. Others favor a pen. These students cross out their mistakes by drawing a thin line through the unwanted word or words. It is as if they still want to keep the words they are tossing away, or perhaps they are not sure about their value and will decide when the work is finished. Sketches and drawings also sometimes appear along with the words.

A few students sit at tablets and tap away at the keyboards. Others stand and write while resting one foot on a swing bar. I pass children who engage in serious conversation in whisper voices. Their eyes light up as they share the words they have written. I can almost feel the flutter of their hearts as they praise and polish each other's work. They are eager to hear what their peers have to say about their work. The writers nod and scribble on sticky notes, sometimes passing these squares to their partner.

The room is filled with writing and whispering voices and charts. As I look around the room, it seems everything is homegrown. A few children approach a chart labeled "Why Authors Use Dialogue" and sit on the rug before it with their notebooks opened. Where is the teacher? Ah, there she is, sitting on the carpet. She, too, is writing in a small notebook. She stops for a moment, looks around the room, and smiles.

*I will come back again tomorrow to observe writing workshop. I must admit, it feels somewhat like a magical experience to me. I feel compelled to share this story with anyone who will listen.*

## What Our Book Has to Offer

We warmly welcome you to experience writing workshop in a new light or for the very first time with our newest adventure in writing, *Welcome to Writing Workshop: Engaging Today's Students with a Model That Works*. This book stems from our heartfelt beliefs about the place of writing workshop in elementary schools. The notion of writing workshop originates from the real-world experiences of writers everywhere. Each student in our classroom is a working author. The teacher is a working author, too, and a coach, guiding young authors as they imagine the possibilities for their craft. A workshop approach is designed to emphasize the act of writing itself—students spend most of their time putting pencil to paper, not just learning about it. Students learn how to find their own topics to write about, because we know choice will help to create engaged writers, not just compliant ones. In writing workshop, students are part of the assessment process as well, managing their own development as they work through a wide variety of writing projects in a sustained and self-directed way.

In a writing workshop classroom, emphasis is placed on sharing work with the class, on peer conferring and editing, and on the collection of a wide variety of work in a writing folder. Teachers write for and with their students, sharing their own work as well. The workshop setting encourages students to develop a writing identity; in other words, they are raising themselves to a conscious level of "I am a writer, and what I have to say is important now." A writing workshop approach helps student writers take their writing seriously, to be engaged rather than simply compliant.

In our book, we offer routines, tips, advice, and resources, as well as short, focused video clips, for teachers in grades K through 6. We know process writing is not a new idea, and yet we do not often see a true writing workshop taking place in many of the classrooms we observe. We hope the video clips do exactly that: offer glimpses into many of the components of a true writing workshop that we discuss in the pages of this book. Video clips appear in chapters and are best viewed while you are reading about their content rather than in isolation. For example, in Chapter 6, "Independent Writing Time," you will find a heading about leading a mid-workshop interruption. If you read the text and then view the video where fourth-grade teacher Catherine Gehman talks about this important strategy, it will make good sense and stay with you. In all of the places where we share a video clip, you'll note that the text explains and the video further illustrates each practice.

We know that having the time to write is crucial for our students, and yet some teachers give away writing time for test preparation or allow students to read their independent reading book. The time to develop as confident, effective writers is too important to give away to other activities. We strongly feel our students need to become competent writers to be able to participate as global citizens. Writing is the most powerful tool we have to think aloud on paper, organize our thoughts, and make our thinking visible and permanent. We know writing workshop is most effective when it occurs daily. Then students know that their teachers and school officials believe that writing is important.

We know teachers do a better job with a writing-workshop approach than any other method. Writing cannot be taught solely from a scripted program. Without a true understanding of the writing workshop approach, teachers have to rely on a one-size-fits-all program format. Although it is comforting to have a script or instructions on what to do each day, teachers must be able to assess student work to make informed and responsive choices about instructional decisions. They must be able to provide high-quality feedback on a regular basis, knowing what to specifically praise and what to work on to move each individual writer forward. Writing workshop asks the students to make deliberate choices about their writing. Choice in writing workshop is as important as choice in reading workshop. This choice will help students be actively engaged, reflect on their growth and set goals, and imitate the writing process of mentor authors.

How can we expect students to produce high-quality writing in the classroom and on standardized test writing prompts without establishing extensive writing routines that give students the models to imitate, time to create and revise, tools to use, and opportunities to choose writing topics they care about? This book discusses how to establish the right environment to grow writers, and how to establish writing workshop procedures, routines, and management practices to use the writing time allowed by your daily schedule most effectively. By breaking down the components of writing workshop and detailing everything from explanations of writing process and writing traits to small-group strategy lessons and minilessons about craft moves, this comprehensive book will provide the know-how you need to feel confident and comfortable as a teacher of writers.

At the end of each chapter is a section called "When You're Ready" that offers another chance to extend your thinking and learning. We hope you will find these sections challenging and rich in possibilities.

## Who Should Read This Book?

*Welcome to Writing Workshop* will help both novice and veteran teachers implement their own workshops in their own classrooms with more confidence. Reading specialists and support teachers can benefit from the experiences and descriptions of key components of writing workshop since they often support struggling readers and writers in small-group situations. This book is for administrators, too, who will observe writing workshops and offer praise and polish. We use our combined years of classroom experience as writing teachers and literacy coaches to share real classroom experiences and validate their suggestions and conclusions. Our study guide to accompany this book is on the Stenhouse website. We hope professional learning communities and teacher-initiated partnerships and book clubs will use our book to grow in confidence and knowledge of how a teacher of writers builds and maintains a community of writers in writing workshop.

Enjoy the journey, and please write along the way. Happy writing (and reading)!

# Chapter 1

# What is Writing Workshop?

## A Guiding Belief: Everyone Can Learn to Write

We've all had students arrive in our classrooms who haven't produced any writing. They come with notes in their files saying, "This student hates to write" or "This student can't write." It's our belief that every student can write—even the ones who have stopped believing in themselves as writers. All students have stories to tell. All students are experts on topics. All students have opinions. We take what children come to us with and help them shape what's inside of them into writing on the page.

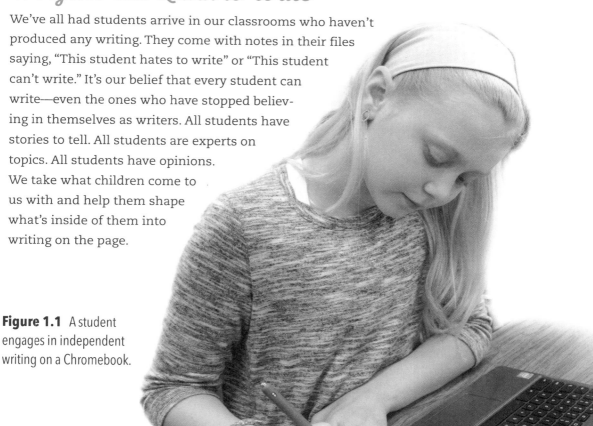

**Figure 1.1** A student engages in independent writing on a Chromebook.

# Writing Workshop Defined

So, what exactly is writing workshop? The act of writing is complex, and so is the instruction writing teachers must provide for all the students who fill today's diverse classrooms. The structure for writing workshop is simple: it is student centered and based on the belief that students become successful writers when they write frequently, for extended periods of time, and on topics of their choice. Yes, it is challenging to keep track of twenty or more writers who are in various places in the writing process and/or who are writing for different audiences and different purposes. Although it may be daunting at times to keep track of everything and meet each writer where they are, the process of writing has similar components. All writers have a purpose for writing and a target audience. Writers make decisions about topic, genre, and form. They may decide along the way to designate this piece as a writer's notebook entry or to carry it through to publication. Student writers may have the option of deciding whether this piece will be submitted for a grade or remain in a showcase portfolio. They also have (or should have) the choice to abandon the piece before completion and start a new one, unless, of course, it is a grade-level benchmark piece or standardized test requirement everyone must complete. In writing workshop, we develop the habits young writers need to form so writing is a routine they value and even enjoy. We work to help writers acquire the cumulative knowledge they need to develop and hone their craft. The focus in writing workshop is entirely on the writer. We help writers develop the skills, strategies, and craft that will sustain them across multiple pieces of writing in various genres.

# When Are We Most Effective in Helping Student Writers Grow?

We believe the way to help students become writers is to work with each child within his or her zone of proximal development, or ZPD. Using the gradual release of responsibility model (i.e., I Do, We Do, You Do), we challenge students to independently try a strategy or craft move, or engage in a task that requires some risk taking on their part after they have watched

**The Exhilaration of Writing Workshop**

http://sten.pub/ww01

*Frank Murphy, sixth-grade teacher*

the teacher model and after they have tried it in a shared or guided experience (see Figure 1.2). In this model, students work with teachers, and sometimes other students and mentor texts, to reach their full potential. Lev Vygotsky's framework helps our students forge new attitudes about writing as they become more courageous and more willing to access new pathways. Thus, the ZPD is where the child can be successful trying a new skill or strategy with the teacher's guidance (Vygotsky 1986). That is also why we need to be teachers of writers who write. We need to write so we can take risks and try new strategies and craft moves, too. As writing teachers who write, we are able to experience the same struggles and attempts to problem solve in order to improve our skills as conferrers. When we confer with students as a mentor author, we have the confidence and practical experience to model writing techniques and confer with students as they move through the writing process, taking risks and experimenting with craft and mechanics.

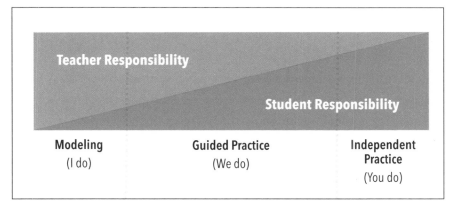

**Figure 1.2** The gradual release of responsibility model of instruction is built on Russian educational theorist Lev Vygotsky's work on zones of proximal development. The responsibility for cognitive work moves slowly from teacher, to a shared responsibility between teachers and students, to independent practice by the students. Emphasis as applied to the writing workshop model is on instruction that mentors students into becoming capable writers when learning and applying new strategies and craft moves they are not yet capable of using independently. The scaffolded model for instruction provides the support students need to be successful.

## Classroom Management and Routines

Writing workshop teachers need an excellent management system. Success depends on the routines that make workshop hum like an efficient hive of honeybees. The success of writing workshop depends on kids having a solid understanding of writing process, the qualities of good writing, and how to continually make reading-writing connections.

## What Else Do Writing Workshop Teachers Need?

Writing workshop teachers need solid knowledge about how to teach writing gleaned from their own ongoing writing experiences, professional texts about the teaching of writing such as this one, and attendance at conferences (local, state, and/or national). The study of mentor texts is essential. Regie Routman (2005) has sound criteria for defining writing workshop:

- Sustained, daily writing on mostly chosen topics
- Writing for purposes and audiences valued by the writer
- Learning craft moves and playing with language
- Learning how to make writing engaging for the reader
- Conferring to respond and celebrate what writers do well and offering a polish—something the writer is ready to try
- Working toward writing fluency and writing accuracy
- Often, publishing for audiences other than the teacher

## Our Writing Classroom Reflects Our Values and Beliefs About How Children Learn

We inform our literacy practices by understanding our belief and value systems, and observe our classroom's physical environment, our routines, and our own writing processes as a writer. A look around a classroom can quickly reveal what is valued: a place to gather the writing community, anchor charts, student writing, a classroom library, easy access to writing materials, and a place to confer and gather feedback. A teacher is moving around the classroom, stopping now and then to chat with a student about his or her writing, then making a few quick notes. Those notes will provide a way to hold students accountable for a goal or goals they will discuss in a teacher-student conference later that day or week. Earlier, the class gathered on the rug to listen to a read-aloud, a book that will become a mentor text for this classroom. Everywhere, purposeful work is going on—both teacher and students are making decisions about what is the essential work for that day.

## Terminology

Before we move forward, let's get on the same page. Here are some common terms we'll use throughout the book:

- **Writing workshop** is a block of time in the school day in which students are actively involved in writing. It begins with a short minilesson, which provides time for the teacher to teach one strategy that will help the students become better writers not just for the piece of writing they're doing on that day, but for the rest of their lives. Next, students have independent writing time, which typically lasts twenty-five to forty-five minutes. The workshop time ends with a five-to-ten-minute share session. The most important thing to remember about writing workshop is that "In the workshop children write about what is alive and vital and real for them—and other writers in the room listen and extend and guide, laugh and cry and marvel" (Calkins 1994, 19).

- **Minilessons** are short (about ten minutes) and explicit sessions where teachers directly instruct students on *one* writing strategy. Minilessons begin with a connection that activates the students' prior knowledge. Next, teachers share the teaching point, which they demonstrate so students understand how to accomplish that strategy. Then, students are given two to three minutes to actively engage with the strategy, having a go with it on their own or with a partner. Teachers walk around the meeting area to see what students are doing and quickly debrief what they notice, or

**A Rationale for Writing Workshop from a Principal's Perspective**

http://sten.pub/ww02

*Maggie Seidel, Principal*

they have one student or pair of students share what they learned. Finally, teachers link the strategy to the work the students will do on that day and every day as writers.

- **Independent writing** time makes up the bulk of the elementary writing workshop, lasting twenty-five to forty-five minutes. Students practice the strategy taught during the minilesson and/or write using other strategies they have learned. Teachers circulate around the classroom to confer with students or to hold strategy lessons during independent writing time.

- **Conferring** takes place during independent writing time. Typically, teachers confer with students one-on-one, but sometimes they may confer with a writing partnership. Teachers have an opportunity to provide highly individualized instruction to a student during a five-minute writing conference where they explicitly teach the writer one new strategy to help them become a better writer (not to improve just the piece of writing the student is working on that day). There are several types of conference formats, which include, but are not limited to, coaching, compliment, mentor text, Research-Decide-Teach, and strategic. Regardless of the conference type, it's important to remember the words of Donald Murray, who wrote, "[Conferences] are not minilectures but the working talk of fellow writers sharing their experience with the writing process. At times, of course, they will be teacher and student, master and apprentice, if you want, but most of the time they will be remarkably close to peers, because each writer, no matter how experienced, begins again with each draft" (2004, 148).

- **Small-group work** meets the needs of multiple students at the same time. Teachers select three to five children who need to receive instruction on the same writing strategy. Teachers may begin with a compliment for the group, but alternatively, they may dive into instructing the students in the strategy so students will have ample time to have a go with the strategy by practicing it in their writing while still in the presence of their teacher.

- **Share sessions** occur during the final five to ten minutes of every writing workshop. Typically, the class returns to the meeting area with their teacher, who has a couple of students showcase their work. The work showcased in the share session could reflect the day's minilesson teaching point or could be something smart the teacher noticed a student doing during a one-on-one writing conference or in a strategy lesson. However, share sessions can also be opportunities for reflection, partner work, or full-class sharing.

- **Teacher-as-Writer** refers to the notion that teachers of writing must be writers themselves. Workshop teachers keep writer's notebooks, which they share on a regular basis with students, and do the same kinds of writing they're asking their students to do. When teachers are writers, it helps them understand their students' struggles with the writing process, since they've grappled with it themselves.

- **Mentor texts** are pieces of writing used with one or more students to lift the level of writing. "Mentor texts help writers notice things about an author's work that is not like anything they might have done before and empower them to try something new" (Dorfman and Cappelli 2007, 3).

- **Writer's notebooks** are tools to help one live a writerly life. These notebooks can be housed in marble composition books, fancy journals, or digital apps (such as Noteshelf or Penultimate). Regardless of the form, writer's notebooks are places where students can practice their writing on a daily basis. Aimee Buckner contends, "A writer's notebook creates a place for students (and writers) to save their words—in the form of a memory, a reflection, a list, a rambling of thoughts, a sketch, or even a scrap of paper taped on the page" (2004, 4). Writer's notebooks are also workbenches allowing young writers to practice strategies presented in minilessons and to experiment with story ideas, language, scenes, or revisions.

## Four Types of Writing

In writing workshop the students' writing often focuses on one type of writing during a unit of study. Curricular demands may require students to write a narrative or an opinion piece. Within the four writing types we describe, students should have choice to decide what to write about. There will be times when we give them prompts; however, students need to learn to make good decisions, including how to find their own topics and purposes for writing.

Within each writing type, teachers and students can make decisions about genres, formats, and even shapes that help us scaffold writing. Each genre, like the four writing types, has characteristics that support the job it is intended to do such as to tell a story or offer an opinion. We often talk about writing as fiction or nonfiction, but in the real world, we have many examples of texts that "mix" the genres. For example, in *Sky Boys: How They Built the Empire State Building* by Deborah Hopkinson, an informational account of the construction of the Empire State Building is framed by a story beginning and ending related in second-person voice to draw the reader in. Narrative writing comprises many subgenres, including folktales, historical fiction, personal narrative, science fiction, and mystery writing. Information writing can include written instructions, reporting, recounting, feature article writing, reports, and biographies. In our daily lives, we write lists as memory jogs, fill out forms and applications, send emails, cards, and letters to friends and family, and sometimes keep a personal diary or journal to record our feelings and daily observations or sometimes to remember our hopes, dreams, and goals.

In writing workshop, we write to communicate our ideas to others; specifically, we find our purpose for writing and our target audience. It is in writing workshop where students gain myriad experiences in writing across the writing types. It is here that our students can concentrate on the act of writing and learn about their own writing process while establishing a writing identity. We want to help our students know themselves as writers. To accomplish this task, we must help them learn about themselves through opportunities to write daily for substantial periods of time in many genres across the writing types. We study mentor texts and include a writerly discussion about the characteristics of the genre and selected lines or passages from the text. Then we model a craft, convention, or structure for our students by imitating the mentor text before asking them to emulate the mentor text.

## NARRATIVE

A narrative tells a story. The writer cannot simply tell what happens. He or she creates the experience through a balance of both showing and telling. Sometimes, a story writer uses flashbacks or foreshadowing. A narrative creates a mood or tone that appeals to the emotions.

Features:

- A single narrator's voice and point of view
- A single event or series of events re-created in chronological order.
- Details about setting, characters, action, and speech that make up that one event
- Words and sentence structures that create a tone and mood appropriate to the event
- A "So what?" for the reader to understand

## INFORMATION

An information piece focuses on explaining an event or experience that has happened or might happen again. The writer analyzes the features and describes or explains the big ideas through examples, specific facts, and specific details.

Features:

- A single writer's voice and point of view
- A single point being made through content organized in a way that meaningfully supports the point (not necessarily in chronological order)
- Content that has been sorted into categories of ideas that explain the point through anecdotes, specific examples, details, and facts

- Words and sentence structures that create a tone appropriate to the point

## OPINION

An opinion piece offers a message expressing a belief or claim about something; it is the expression of a belief that is held with confidence and often substantiated by knowledge (experience) or proof (citing experts). The focus is linked with a target audience, and the content must be audience appropriate. The writer's job is to offer his or her opinion in a logical, meaningful way.

Features:

- A single writer's voice and point of view on an issue
- A single point being argued through content organized in a meaningful way that supports the point
- Content that has been sorted into reasons that support the arguments through specific examples, anecdotes, facts, details, quotes from experts, statistics, and additional analysis that may include further explanation
- Words, sentence structures, and rhetorical devices that create a tone appropriate to the point and the target audience

## POETRY

Poetry is drawing a picture with words. Poetry takes many forms and often has a rhyme pattern, although some poems do not use rhyme.

Features:

- The easiest way to recognize poetry is that it is usually written in stanzas. Whereas other types of writing are most often organized with sentences and paragraphs, poetry is normally organized into *lines*.
- Poems communicate through the way the words sound and the way the poem looks on the page. White space, verses, and line breaks are important. Poets use the sounds of consonants and vowels to create

emotion. Rhyme, the absence of rhyme, alliteration, assonance, and consonance help the writer play with language.

- An important characteristic of poetry is concentrated language and economy of expression. Words serve many purposes—to convey meaning and to convey feeling. Every word counts and almost all nonessential words have been eliminated.

- Although poems make good sense, they also often work at an emotional or irrational level, too. What causes the strongest emotions is not what the poem describes, but often what it causes the reader to imagine.

## Mentor Texts

Mentor texts are examples of exemplary writing that can be studied to lift the level of student writing. As Tom Newkirk describes, "A great mentor text does more than show us qualities of good writing. It provokes something in us—memory, passion, a desire to write, to take our turn" (2018). Once students are shown how to read like a writer (Ray 1999), mentor texts can become powerful teaching tools. We believe there are three distinct types of mentor texts—published, student written, and teacher written—that can be used with students.

- Published mentor texts are written by writers who have gone through the publication process (i.e., worked with an editor) with traditional and nontraditional publishing options outside of school. Published texts can include, but are not limited to, books, articles, and short stories. Most often, in elementary school classrooms, mentor texts are fiction and nonfiction picture books that showcase the qualities of good writing to students. Teachers may also share and study books of poetry, short stories, or middle-grade novels alongside students in minilessons, strategy lessons, or conferences.

- Student-written mentor texts are pieces of writing created by children. Typically, they're written by a teacher's former students and shared with future classes. These student-written pieces can come from any stage of the writing process (e.g., notebook entries,

**Read-Alouds Are Essential to Writing Workshop**

http://sten.pub/ww03

*Lisa Jacobs, third-grade teacher*

first drafts, published pieces) so students can have a vision of the type of writing they're expected to accomplish. Many teachers have children at several levels of sophistication whose work they regularly keep and archive during each unit of study for the purpose of using it with students at varying stages of development in the future. Students are often inspired by the work of mentor authors who are students from their own class as well as students from a previous year's class. Studying the work of other student writers at their same grade level is highly motivating. It helps create an "I can do that" attitude!

- Teacher-written mentor texts are crafted by teachers in service of the units of study they are teaching. Writing you do—at any stage of the writing process—can be held up as a mentor text for students since you are the living, breathing author who can discuss the moves you made right there in front of your students. Some teachers craft mentor texts for their students using the mirror writing concept (Cruz 2015) so their demonstration text is accessible to their students.

> *The way mirror writing typically goes is that teachers choose a piece of student writing that is typical of many students in her class. She then spends some time reading the piece very closely and looking for what the student is doing as a writer. Not looking at what is absent. Looking at what is present. There's a reason for this. We can't mirror something that is not there, only what is there. Then, the teacher usually thinks of a topic she can write about that is different but can hit the same points the student hits (137).*

By using mirror writing, a teacher can create a piece of writing tailored to a student's ability level, thereby making it an accessible demonstration text.

It is important to note the difference between touchstone texts and mentor texts. "Touchstone texts are books, articles, short stories or poems that

**Give Yourself Classroom Cred with Your Writers**

http://sten.pub/ww04

*Frank Murphy, sixth-grade teacher*

you use with your entire class. These are utilized during the demonstration of your minilessons and/or are read alouds that the whole class can draw on. Mentor texts can be used in two different ways. First, a mentor text can be used to lift the level of a child's writing. Second, a mentor text is not always used with an entire class of kids. Sometimes you might use a mentor text with just one or two students" (Shubitz 2009, 24). However, the most important purpose of a mentor text is to set students up for future writing success:

> *Mentor texts empower students to become independent, which is crucial because they will not always have you as their writing teacher. If students develop an understanding of how to tap into the power of mentor texts, they will be able to seek out their own mentors in the future. When they go off into the world, they will be confronted with many types of writing tasks. What a gift we give them when they know how to notice what is striking about an author's writing and develop theories about why an author writes a particular way. Then they are able to translate their observations into sophisticated craft moves on their own. (Ayres and Shubitz 2010, 142)*

## Writing Processes

Writers work through stages of prewriting (generating, collecting, and nurturing), drafting, revising, editing, publishing, and reflecting in a recursive process, often building in opportunities to confer with peers (or their editors) along the way. Although writers rarely take a linear approach, we still see evidence of this routine in elementary classrooms. The recursive process is a chaotic one, often beginning with a gathering of materials, a search for a topic—an idea, a word, a phrase, a sentence, a familiar quote— anything that will help one get started! When teachers talk about writing process to their students, they are trying to describe what writers do in the real world. Truth be told, we cannot talk about "the writing process" since writers tend to have different pathways that work best for them. Thus, we need to talk about writing processes. One way to help students understand

The Writing Process Isn't Linear. So Why Do Schools Keep Pretending That It Is?

writing process is to hold a writerly conversation after students have talked with a partner and/or jotted some notes about the way they went about creating the last piece of writing that was ready to be published in some format. As you rove about the classroom, you can also make some notes of writerly behaviors you've observed. You will discover both similarities and differences about the way your students write. That's a worthwhile starting point. It is good to remember that writing fluency—getting it down—is the first consideration for our elementary school writers. Then, we can talk about form and correctness. The following description is the anatomy of the writing process. It is important to remember that a return to planning (collecting and nurturing) can occur at any point in the process, just as revision can occur as early as the initial planning stage. The Common Core emphasizes the importance of process as well as product, and Graham and Harris (2014) suggest that teaching strategies for planning, revising, and editing text can be an effective way to help students use the process to be more successful.

**Planning** refers to preliminary work, a rehearsal or warm-up for the writing. Planning (sometimes referred to as collecting or prewriting) activities include sketching, observing, reading about topics, rereading a mentor text, talking with a partner, examining photos, responding to writing crafted by the teacher or another adult, researching on the Internet, webbing, mapping, using other graphic organizers, interviewing, and soaking up the world around us. Everything around us can offer writers prewriting experiences. We just have to practice observing our world carefully and intentionally. Talking is an important part of this stage of the process. Oral rehearsal, talking about what we are going to write about, is especially important for our youngest writers. In fact, sometimes, planning involves only talking about our writing. We do not always have to write. Collecting helps a student find ideas and topics to write about. In minilessons, teachers can introduce a variety of strategies designed to help students find topics and generate, shape, and clarify ideas. Writers need a repertoire of prewriting strategies and should be able to determine which ones might be most helpful for their purposes for writing and the topics they choose.

**Drafting** gets the ideas from mind to paper (or screen) as quickly as possible so ideas are not lost. The emphasis here is on content, not correctness. Writers should compose without undue concern for mechanics or spelling. Encourage students to cross out rather than erase as they are creating the first draft so that they can retrieve ideas if need be. It may help students to write on every other line so they can revise more easily at a later point. Although writing fluency is important to the draft stage, some students may find it easier to revise and/or edit as they go along, sometimes dividing a piece into a beginning, a middle, and an end.

**Revision** addresses what is working and what isn't. It is a way of re-seeing or re-imagining the writing piece. Writers examine their drafts and decide whether they should or want to make changes. Often, revision work follows a teacher or peer conference. A good strategy for revision is to first examine the writing for focus. Does it stay on topic and have a point? Next, look closely at the content. Can the writer add to it, delete from it, rearrange or replace words or phrases, or substitute strong, specific words for weak ones?

**Editing** is often saved for the final read(s) but can happen at any stage of the writing process. When the writer is satisfied that a piece of writing makes sense and says what he wants it to say, and when he has developed the content as best he can, it is time to focus on correctness. The writer should be held accountable for making corrections in spelling, punctuation, capitalization, and grammar to the best of his ability. Our youngest writers may work on spacing, end punctuation, and letter formation. Inventive spelling is acceptable, but students can be accountable for environmental print and sight words they have learned. In a conference, a teacher may ask the student to work on a convention or grammar issue. Here, it is important to remember that proofreading is difficult even for experienced writers. We cannot ask our young writers to fix everything.

**Publishing** can take many forms: individual student books, class books, classroom newsletters, blog entries on a classroom website, articles for community papers, scripts, letters enclosed in envelopes and mailed, postcards, emails, entries in online writing contests, and author-of-the-week bulletin board displays. It is important that teachers provide students with frequent opportunities to publish their writing. Publishing serves as a great motivator! Sometimes, a publishing conference with a teacher or other adult precedes the act of publishing.

## Sharing and Reflecting Happen Throughout the Writing Process

Sharing gives students a chance to read their writing to a peer and to their teacher and ask for feedback. Ralph Fletcher and Joann Portalupi (2001) suggest that the peer or teacher read to the writer so the writer can be the first person to respond in a conference. Sharing time can be about giving the writer a chance to hear his writing for the first time as it is read aloud to him. The writer can also share the piece, sometimes posing a question or questions such as, "Is my beginning interesting? Does it make you want to hear more?" Sharing can occur at any time—as early as the planning stage or before a first draft is completed. Sharing our writing in the last few minutes of workshop can be related to reflections. Students will not have time to read their entire piece, but they can share revisions to leads, endings, content, and even organizational structures. Sometimes, we can ask our students to share the best sentence they wrote in workshop and explain why they chose it. Students may even have guest author spots in a partner classroom at the same grade level or a different one. A "student of the week" can highlight his or her writing on a special bulletin board and read from the place of honor, "the author's chair." The purpose of writing is to communicate ideas to others; it is crucial to give student writers the time to share their writing. Sharing is a big part of the joy in writing workshop!

Throughout the writing process, students will have many opportunities for reflection. The questions we ask our students during conferences are the same questions we hope they will ask themselves in self-conferences, which we discuss in greater detail in Chapter 7, "Conferring." Students can use their writer's notebook to reflect on a goal set in a conference or use a checklist or rubric to reflect on their learning. *Have I used new craft moves that helped my writing? How did they make my writing better? What mentor text can I return to for some help with descriptions . . . Creating an anecdote? Using transition words?* Although reflection often comes after a piece has been published, it can be used to make changes.

A final word: Not all drafts will be taken through each step of the writing process. Many will not warrant the time and attention final drafts demand. However, students should be familiar with their writing process and many strategies for planning, revising, editing, publishing, and reflection.

## Final Thoughts

Writing workshop is more than a philosophy. It is an efficient model for teaching writers. The workshop model allows teachers to create frameworks for individualized, small-, and whole-group instruction, as well as for formative assessment. It works because workshop is rooted in the notion that everyone is a writer and that writers need time to write frequently—daily—if at all possible, for extended periods and (for the most part) on topics of their own choosing.

Lucy Calkins (2018) says there are three levels of a writing workshop. Level one is the *pulling teeth* level, which is a start-and-stop writing workshop filled with worksheets and material found on a variety of paid Internet sites. Level two is the *good student* level, which is where one can see what the teacher taught each day. The kids do what they're told and no more. This level is more about compliance than about engagement. Level three is the *all-in* level where the "work bristles with deep feeling and intimacy." Children aren't just good students, they are writers. Through the pages of this book, it is our hope that we help you reach a level three, ALL IN, writing workshop!

## When You're Ready

Now that you've read our first chapter, take some time to think about what your writing time looks like and feels like. What are your beliefs about writing? What do you value? Then, look at the following list adapted from Richard Bullock's *Why Workshop? Changing Course in 7–12* (1998, 2). Where do

**Creating a District-Wide Culture of Writing**
http://sten.pub/ww05

*Betsy Gunsalus, Director of Elementary Curriculum and Student Assessment*

**The Uniqueness of the Workshop Model**
http://sten.pub/ww06

*Melissa Schmitz, Instructional Coach*

you place yourself right now? Are you a traditionalist? Are you straddling the line between a traditional writing classroom and a writing workshop model? Are you ready to try something new and exciting?

| Traditional | Workshop |
|---|---|
| • The teacher, school district, or state designs and implements the curriculum. | • Teacher and students negotiate curriculum, both individually and in groups (within mandated constraints). |
| • Students practice skills and memorize facts, often using workbooks and worksheets. | • Students actively construct knowledge—the concepts and meanings. |
| • Content is broken down into discrete, sequential units over lengthy lessons that often take the lion's share of workshop time. | • Content is presented whole, in meaningful contexts through short minilessons, writerly classroom conversations, and an inquiry approach. |
| • Largely, the way students learn writing strategies is through whole-group instruction. | • Processes (planning, drafting, multiple drafts for revision and editing; self-evaluation and reflection) are valued as much as the products themselves. |
| • Writing topics and writing prompts are assigned with little attention to choice. | • Taking educated risks is valued. Writers grow because they try new strategies, craft moves, and organizational scaffolds. |
| • Products are the focus—the result is more important than the process. | • Choice, collaboration, and challenge are greatly valued. |
| • Avoiding mistakes is important. | • Instruction is presented in whole-group and small-group formats, partnerships, and one-on-one conferring. |
| • Summative assessment is valued highly, and almost everything is graded. | • Some writing, such as the writing in a writer's notebook, is not assigned a grade. |
| • Teachers are in charge of evaluating and grading. | • Students are assessed by their performances on meaningful tasks, often through portfolios of their work, in conferences, and through daily formative assessment that includes record-keeping such as anecdotal records, checklists, and audiotapes. |
| • Learning is uniform. | • Students learn how to reflect on their practices, set goals, and self-assess. |
| • Expectations are fairly uniform for all students, with no evidence of small-group or product differentiation. | • Students sometimes do the teaching, partnering with a peer or with the teacher. During share sessions and mid-workshop interruptions, students can offer valuable tips and suggestions: a noticing, an approach to a problem, a topic worth exploring, or scaffolds for organization. |
| | • Learning is expected to be individual and unique. Students are encouraged to imagine the possibilities! |
| | • Evaluation is oriented toward success. Students are expected to create something concrete during workshop time. |

# Chapter 2

# The "Write" Environment

## Creating Our Classrooms

I f you're like us, you are the kind of teacher who starts thinking about the next school year in June. It's perfectly normal to think about every-thing from desk arrangements to how you will use bulletin board space weeks before your new group of children arrives for the first day of school. If you're a general elementary school teacher, you have to design your classroom to be functional for all subject areas. However, there are some specific things to think about—with regard to writing workshop—when you're preparing your room for the new school year.

## Furniture

### STUDENT SEATING

Some teachers seat students at tables, whereas others have students seated at individual desks. Your students can still be seated in coopera-tive groupings even if you have desks. We suggest pushing desks together into clusters of four so children are sitting with a small group of peers, rather than sitting in rows. In classrooms we've observed, some teachers have written grants to their education foundations, on DonorsChoose, or to home and school associations to acquire a variety of seating options, slanted desks, and standing desks with a single bar for students to rest one foot. Proper posture can be promoted with the use of child-size balance-ball chairs with removable backrests. Children who have learning differences or conditions such as attention-deficit hyperactivity disorder, may find a yoga ball with a base or a wobble chair helpful to focus their attention while seated.

## Around the Classroom

Many teachers have bean bags, benches, large pillows, or cozy chairs for students to use during independent writing time. In many classrooms, only the general meeting area has a rug. Some teachers use carpet remnants (little squares) that students can use when finding a seat on the tiled floor. It helps to have a central place to store these items when students aren't using them.

## Meeting Area

We believe the meeting area, which is where you'll gather your students for minilessons, read-alouds, and full-class share sessions, should be the focal point of your classroom. A meeting area starts with a place to sit, usually a large, colorful rug. Some teachers may have benches or other seating around the perimeter of the meeting area. There should be an easel with chart paper and markers, an interactive whiteboard or screen (with computer), a document camera, and other supplies you may need for on-the-spot revision or editing (such as scissors, tape, glue sticks, sticky notes, and writing utensils). Be sure there's a clearly defined path for students to use to get to and depart from the meeting area.

## Writing Center

It's important to have a well-stocked writing center that students are taught to care for and restock. Here are some items you might put in your classroom's writing center:

- Writing utensils (e.g., colored pencils, crayons, highlighters, markers, pencils, pens)
- Sticky notes, spider legs, or index cards to help with revision

- Hole punch, mistake remover, scissors, staplers, tape
- Variety of paper—different colors, sizes, and styles
- Reference materials (e.g., dictionaries, thesauruses, books on writing)
- Date stamp
- Calendar
- Mentor texts
- Small versions of class-created checklists and charts

## Mentor Text Sets

In a perfect world, you'll have several copies of each published mentor text you will use with your students. However, we realize this is challenging because of the cost of purchasing books—even when they're released in paperback. Therefore, be sure to place mentor texts on your wish list for holiday gifts or a contribution to the classroom library from a school book fair. Borrow copies from other grade-level partners whenever possible. Sign out copies from the school and public libraries. Write a grant to your home and school association (HSA) or parent-teacher organization (PTO) for mentor text sets. Some school districts offer grants through their education foundation. Collaborate with grade-team partners to place mentor text sets on the building order for books/ textbooks/supplies for the new school year. There are many ways to get the funds for additional mentor texts for your classroom library.

Whether you have a big budget for multiple copies of mentor texts or have just one copy, what matters most is making mentor texts accessible to students so they can access them any time they need inspiration during writing workshop.

## Focus Spots

Not every child writes best at a desk, which is why it's important to allow students to have a space in the classroom where they feel comfortable enough to write while still being productive. You can allow students to choose their own "focus spots" (Ayres and Shubitz 2010).

Early in the year, allow students to try different places in the classroom where they will sit (or stand!) for independent writing. At the end of the first week of school, ask each child to give you their top focus spot preferences. Then assign spots to each child so they will have a place of their own that they'll head to for independent writing as soon as each minilesson concludes.

Sometimes the spots children choose don't work for them. Work with them to find a better focus spot so they can be more productive during independent writing time.

## Displays

### ANCHOR CHARTS

If you teach multiple content areas, you might color-code the anchor charts (e.g., black ink for writing, blue for reading, green for math). From there, you can designate bulletin board space for each subject area in your classroom. The combination of color-coded charts and special wall space for each subject area makes it easy for students to access co-created writing charts in the classroom.

### MENTOR AUTHOR BOARD

Many writing teachers have invisible coteachers who help them lift the level of their students' writing on a regular basis. We can celebrate the things mentor authors teach our students to do by including snippets of text from a mentor text a student studied and posting it alongside the writing the child did that was inspired by the mentor author. Another option is to post "powerful sentences" that student peers notice while conferring with a partner. This way we honor both the student writer and his peer who notices a craft move or strategy used to make the sentence work.

**Cover the Walls with What You Absolutely Need**

http://sten.pub/ww07

*Catherine Gehman, fourth-grade teacher*

## Work in Progress

It's wise to have a space for students' in-progress work during a unit of study. You can photocopy smart work students are doing and display it on a work-in-progress bulletin board for their peers to see. Some things you might wish to display on a board are the following:

- Craft moves students tried by studying a mentor text
- Strategies students tried—as a result of a one-to-one conference or minilesson—that made their writing stronger (You could display a before and after of the same paragraph.)
- Revisions students made that were an outgrowth of a share session with one of their peers

## Work Stations

There have been debates in the education community for years about whether teachers should have a desk. Stacey got rid of her desk after a year, but found that her conference table turned into a makeshift desk. Eventually, she realized it was time to bring back the desk—as a place to store personal items, not to sit at during the day—since the conference table, which was supposed to be used for working with kids, had become cluttered with her personal effects. The decision of whether you have a desk in your classroom is a matter of personal choice.

You'll need to think about some other things when planning your classroom.

## Conference Table

Many teachers have a circular or U-shaped table where they hold conferences or meet with small groups of students. The location of this table in the classroom is important. We think it should be placed near the center of the room, rather than in a corner, so you can continue to monitor the rest of your students while you work with one or more children at the table.

## Peer Conference Spaces

It's important to have a place for writing partnerships to work together during independent writing time. Since most of your students will be working independently, it's wise to place a couple of peer conference spaces in the far corners of your classroom (if you have flexibility with space). This way, each partnership can work together using soft voices and not disrupt their classmates who are working independently. Since many teachers like silence or a quiet hum during independent writing time, it's wise to place peer conference spaces away from the majority of children's focus spots so the partnerships who are meeting do not disrupt their classmates who are working independently.

## The Social-Emotional Environment

Establishing a writing workshop begins with the work we do to help our students feel safe and secure. We create a social environment where students can share their struggles with others and benefit from listening in to acquire the problem-solving methods of their peers. Teachers must make a conscious effort to work with their students to develop this nurturing writing community where students can talk about what's not working and positively critique their own work and the work of their peers. Perhaps a great way to begin writing workshop is to ask students to think about and then describe a time when they were writing and did not want to stop—when they felt excited and the most important thing was the work they were doing. After they share with a partner, ask them to write or draw about that time or make audio recordings to share every so often during whole-group reflection time. Focusing on aspects of the social-emotional environment is an important part of creating a student-centered workshop and the "write" environment for our student authors.

**The Social-Emotional Environment Begins with the Teacher**
http://sten.pub/ww08

*Frank Murphy, sixth-grade teacher*

## Creating a Safety Net

To have such a community, students must be comfortable with talking about the problems that occur when drafting, revising, and editing and learn how to disagree agreeably with peers. They need to be able to confront problems head-on and feel safe enough to talk about areas of frustration and confusion, what they usually do when problems occur, how strategies and mentor texts helped them solve their problems, and how well these strategies or craft moves worked for them. In a nutshell, they have to feel safe to ask for help and freely share their writing.

## Fostering Engagement

How can we foster engagement in writing workshop? The key to engagement lies in motivation. Motivation to write is linked to many factors, including a student's cultural, gender, and social identity. If, for example, a student's family frowns upon using free time to write a graphic novel instead of playing a sport, or if a student's family rewards the student who does well in school and achieves academic success, then engagement in writing workshop can be affected in either a negative or positive way. Some peer cultures could define writing in negative ways, and for those students, generating interest in writing is critical. Choice in topic and genre is an important factor in motivation. Giving students opportunities to write that graphic novel or poetry anthology in a few regularly scheduled open workshop cycles in a given year is an easy way to honor student interest and provide choice. Even within a narrative unit of study, each writer can choose his own topic—a story he wants to tell. The whole class does not have to write a story about "My Most Embarrassing Moment." If you read *Alexander and the Terrible, Horrible, No Good, Very Bad Day* by Judith Viorst as a read-aloud, some students may want to write their own "Terrible, Horrible, No Good Day" story. Students should have the option to write something different, as long as they are writing a narrative. If you want students to try effective repetition like that used in this story, which is predictable and fun for the reader, you can also

Letting Go and
Providing Students
with Choices

http://sten.pub/ww09

Lisa Jacobs,
*third-grade teacher*

show other mentor texts that use it in different ways. For example, it can also be found in *Fireflies!* by Julie Brinckloe. Additionally, there are many subgenres to introduce to students who are writing story. Depending on a student's grade level and writing interests, perhaps a student wants to write historical fiction, science fiction, or realistic fiction. Students need choice for topic and genre!

Perhaps the most important way to engage students is to make sure they have a writing identity in place. Focusing on an increased awareness of "I am a writer" at a very conscious level is both helpful and necessary. We make an effort to invite our students to discover and revise their writing goals, think about their likes and dislikes, notice where their attention is when they write, identify all the different processes that go on while they write, and prioritize what they value. As they gain a sense of themselves as writers, they become more willing to work hard, persist when struggles arise, and gain confidence in taking risks and trying new approaches and strategies.

## How Can We Build Writer Confidence?

Extending the range of what students can write is a good way to build writer confidence. Introduce them to many genres and a wide range of mentor texts:

- poems
- song lyrics
- book and movie reviews
- how-to manuals
- advertisements
- travel guides
- letters

- web pages
- riddles
- comic strips
- birthday cards (and other celebratory cards)
- notes from friends

Students can share their mentor authors and the mentor texts they are finding and using with classmates. Early in the year, ask students to make a simple list of the kinds of reading and writing they are doing. Have them share in small groups and return to these lists the next month to add to them. We need to convince our struggling and reluctant writers that they are familiar and comfortable with many text types already! This knowledge will help them gain the confidence they'll need to try new organizational patterns and text types.

## Creating a Set of Standards

Teachers can help create a safe environment by agreeing on a set of standards or rules to live by during writing workshop. They model respectful, supportive interactions with others and insist that their students also be respectful and supportive of others. An emotional attachment to teachers, peers, and school itself is vital to student success. Supportive relationships within the writing community (teacher-student, peer-peer, student–mentor author) help students persist when problems arise. Rules to live by in workshop should be created with the students and involve acceptable ways to respond to writing that critique the writing and not the writer. Posting them in the classroom in a prominent location is helpful. Keep them simple to read and easy to understand. Here are two charts used in a third-grade class for both reading and writing workshop and across the day (see Figures 2.1 and 2.2).

**Figure 2.1** Discussion guidelines chart

## Discussion Guidelines Chart

- Stick to the topic.
- Pay attention to the person talking.
- Say something positive (praise) first to link with someone else's thinking.
- Ask questions about ideas given.
- Give everyone a chance to participate.
- Show respect for your peers.
- Try not to interrupt others.

**Figure 2.2** Group thinking questions for whole-class response to writing

## Group Thinking Questions for Whole-Class Response to Writing

- What is the text about?
- What parts do you especially like?
- What suggestions, questions, or comments would you have for the author?
- How can you present this text to your classmates?
- What is your/the author's focus or message?
- Why did you/the author write this piece?

Remember, it is important to talk about what makes writers feel safe enough to ask questions, share their writing, and talk about their confusion. In this type of safe environment, a community is formed where teachers also have many opportunities to share their expertise. They can also point to students' successes and risks to try new things throughout workshop time so students begin to clearly see that different students bring different valuable resources that shape the way they create a text.

## Self-Reflection and Goal-Setting

The small day-to-day decisions readers and writers make require the ability to create short- and long-term goals. Identifying personal goals will help students prioritize and plan. Quiet periods for self-reflection can be built into writing workshop. Goal-setting conferences where the teacher can assist in identifying the steps necessary to achieve the goal are helpful. As students become more mature, a timetable for those steps can help them self-regulate, evaluating their progress and making necessary adjustments to meet their goals. If we want our students to be reflective, however, we need to model reflective thinking practices for them. We can pose a question or two for students to ponder and be prepared to discuss at the end of workshop. Gathering the community for about five minutes to bring closure to workshop is the perfect time to bring your own writing to the whole-group meeting and share your reflection process. If the question is about your lead—whether to begin with a description of setting or character or jump right into the action, for example—you can talk about what made you choose one craft move over another. Gathering the writing community together for this kind of talk at the end of each workshop has big payoffs. Students' confidence and self-esteem increase as they heighten their awareness of their process, concentrating on the "whys" of decision making.

## Opening Our Minds to Let Other People's Thinking In

Finally, we want our students to notice the successful writing behaviors of their peers and teachers. Particularly, we want our writers to notice the ways in which different writers problem-solve, think aloud, and use strategies to improve their writing. The next step is to see the evidence of transfer—where we can see that our writers are benefiting from these writerly conversations with partners, small groups, or in the whole group by trying different approaches and craft moves other writers use to revise and edit their texts.

## Get Inspired

We're inspired by beautiful classrooms that provide flexible seating options for children (see Figures 2.3–2.19). Here is a peek into some of our favorite spaces:

**Figure 2.3** This is one of two meeting areas in an integrated coteaching, or ICT, first-grade classroom.

**Figure 2.4** Some teachers purchase a variety of mobile seating options for students to sit on during minilessons.

**Figure 2.5** Scoop chairs are one of many flexible seating options for young children.

**Figure 2.6** This first-grade classroom has a variety of seating options for children who like to be close to the floor.

**Figure 2.7** A variety of writing surfaces, including slanted desks, provide young writers with a different angle to try while working.

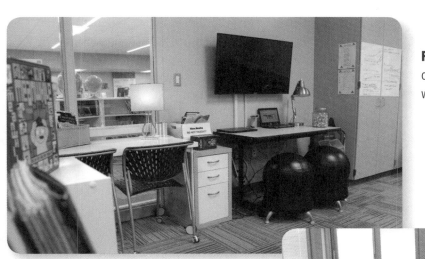

**Figure 2.8** This fifth-grade classroom has a collaboration station with gumdrop chairs.

**Figure 2.9** Collaboration—in small groups or partnerships—can occur when these ottomans, footrests, crates with fabric covers, and a couch are reconfigured. Most of this furniture is light, which makes it easy for the third-grade students who use it to create different seating choices around the classroom.

**Figure 2.10** A third-grade classroom uses flexible seating and a variety of options when it comes time to write. Node chairs and a hexagon-shaped table allow for collaboration in partnerships and small groups.

**Figure 2.11** Rolling chairs and tables call to some writers who like to sit at low tables, whereas high tables with backless stools beckon other students. Node chairs are also available. Fifth graders who like their feet touching the floor can choose among "typical" seating options, too.

**Figure 2.12** Fifth-grade students enjoy having a variety of writing surfaces and seating options, including cozy chairs.

**Figure 2.13** This fifth-grade classroom's peer conferring space is reminiscent of a café.

**Figure 2.14** Students in this third-grade classroom choose this cozy nook when they wish to have a peer conference with their writing partner.

**Figure 2.15** Kindergartners can easily access this low-to-the-ground writing center, which is filled with different kinds of paper, revision tools, and writing utensils.

**Figure 2.16** This upper-grade writing center is filled with a variety of paper choices, supplies, and reference books.

**Figure 2.17** Kindergarten students can access anchor charts, at eye level, that they created with their teacher around the classroom.

**Figure 2.18** Fourth graders showcase their work in progress on a classroom bulletin board.

### Our Learning Space by Cary S. Harrod, fifth-grade teacher

Having done a great deal of research on the impact environment plays on learning, I set about to create a learning space that supports new ways of learning, provides flexibility to reflect the various learners in our space, and is welcoming to all who inhabit it. Upon entering the space, your first impression will be how "unlike" a classroom it looks. Gone are the desks in a row, all facing the front of the room. Instead, you will find a variety of seating options, including node chairs, stools, rocking chairs, beach chairs, chairs on wheels, gumdrop seats, a couch . . . most of which are on casters to allow for flexible learning.

You will also see tables of different shapes and heights: low-to-the-ground, standard height, and high café tables. Four of the tables have writable surfaces, providing students with more opportunities to make their learning visible. For those wishing to work independently, students can choose a node chair with an attached table that can easily be moved when the learning calls for collaboration.

Our space has whiteboards across two walls; one of the boards has a short throw projector to showcase student reading and writing. A soft light has been added to produce a calming effect; a room diffuser sends beautiful scents into the air. If you were to visit our learning space, you would probably hear instrumental music playing softly in the background. For those desiring an even quieter environment, students are encouraged to wear headphones.

*Cary S. Harrod,*
*fifth-grade teacher*

**Figure 2.19** Fifth-grade teacher Cary S. Harrod reflects on the importance of creating an inviting environment for writing workshop that is welcoming to all students.

## Final Thoughts

A literacy-rich environment for writing may include, but is not limited to, classroom libraries that contain a variety of genres and text types and copies of mentor texts (the books the teacher uses for minilessons and read-alouds), anchor charts—teacher-made and co-created with students—and word walls. There are nooks for conferring and working collaboratively, and areas in which to store supplies and writing folders that students can access without the teacher's help. Teachers of writers design and organize their classroom environment to help children get their work done. Comfortable furniture that fits the needs of the students and regular routines instills a feeling of continuity as well as fosters active engagement through choice, a spirit of camaraderie, and active listening. All these things support and sustain the writing community that will help your writers grow and flourish.

## When You're Ready

Classrooms have many distractions. Keep an observation sheet every so often of the number of interruptions and distractions that occur across the day: visits from other teachers, administrators, and students; announcements over the public address system; phone calls; and recess and lunch bells. How can you eliminate some of these interruptions? During read-aloud time and independent writing, consider posting a note on your door asking visitors to return at another time in the day. When you are on the phone or speaking to another teacher, does your workshop keep humming or does it come to a stop? We suggest eliminating some distractions we self-create. For example, we should try to avoid situations like stopping instruction to discipline a student or students and wait for his attention and everyone else's attention. If it's a minor behavior problem, perhaps it can be dealt with later or perhaps you can establish a signal or some other routine that will curb unnecessary disruptive behavior. Set guidelines for "What We Can Do During Writing Workshop" and post it. Assign writing directors each marking period who can answer questions or model what to do during conferences and independent writing time or how to use the publishing center.

# Chapter 3

# A Community of Writers

## The Ingredients for Building and Sustaining Success

## Writing Community

Building a writing community starts in September, but sustaining the community is a yearlong effort. It starts with the teacher and important, achievable goals: to build and sustain a classroom writing community that fosters trust among students and to clearly establish shared values about good writing, the work that writers do, and respect for others' work. We communicate our desire for a community of writers by addressing students as writers during the minilessons, mid-workshop interruption, and share session. We want our students to understand writing is not accomplished in isolation; there is a writing team made up of the entire classroom of writers. Appropriating problem-solving strategies and craft moves from classmates will be key factors in the writing successes of each and every student. To firmly establish a community of writers, students will need daily time for uninterrupted writing, time to talk about their writing processes, time for writerly conversations, time for conferring and collaboration, and time for reflection. Although mentor texts and mentor authors will help students grow as writers, they must also view their own work as important and necessary to move their writing community forward (Dorfman and Cappelli 2017). Finding out how students see themselves as writers is essential. Are they fearful, afraid to make mistakes? Do they see writing as a joyful time in their school day? Understanding our students' attitudes and our own views on writing will help us begin to build a strong writing community.

## Student and Teacher Attitudes

The great Donald Graves (1982) gave us this insightful knowledge: "Children want to write. They want to write the first day they attend school. This is no accident. Before they went to school they marked up walls, pavements, newspapers with crayons, chalk, pens, or pencils . . . anything that made a mark. The child's marks say, 'I am'" (3).

Writing is important. By writing down our thoughts, we can remember them and share them with others. But we can also listen closely to our classmates, family members, and friends. Writing is a lifelong activity that shapes our attitudes and helps us grow as world citizens, too. Often, however, we meet students who are reluctant to write. They sit in our classrooms every year, writers who have become discouraged before they reach us. Maybe they received too many criticisms and were asked to meet too many goals. Perhaps they were never allowed to write in the format or genre that interested them. Maybe they were not introduced to a mentor author who could help spur them on to take risks. Maybe they were just plain scared of being wrong. If we don't help these writers establish a clear writing identity, they will still be reluctant and struggling writers when they leave us in June. In *A Closer Look: Learning More About Our Writers with Formative Assessment K–6*, Dorfman and Dougherty (2017) explain that students cannot be joyful if they are only compliant. Students who are engaged can find the joy in growing as a writer, trying out new strategies and genres, and sharing their writing with myriad audiences. The authors suggest that teachers observe their students closely during writing workshop and complete an engagement inventory to discover how their students use their workshop time (see Figure 3.1). Here is their example:

Our goal for writing workshop participation is total immersion in the writing process. Teachers who make time to find out about their students'

**Ways to Build a Writing Community**

http://sten.pub/ww10

*Lesley Turner, fifth-grade teacher*

# Engagement Inventory from *A Closer Look*

1. Is [ <u>student name</u> ] writing during workshop time? If not, what is he doing?

2. Does this student write at other times across the day when there is opportunity to do so?

3. Does the student find the best spot in the room where he can concentrate while drafting?

4. Is the student working alone all or most of the time or with a partner? When is he more comfortable?

5. Is she "reading the room" (using environmental print) for help with spelling?

6. Does the student stop writing when she is trying to spell a word to wait for help before writing anything else?

7. Does he page through writer's notebook entries to reread or add to a list (for example, expert list, heart map, writing territories, words that describe a season)?

8. Is he producing the same amount of writing most of the students in your class are able to do? More? Less? Explain.

9. Does she do any prewriting? If a plan is developed, is it used?

10. Does he confer with a partner?

11. Does she move closer to an anchor chart to make use of it?

12. How does this student spend his time in workshop? Drawing pictures for a writing piece? Reading a mentor text? Reading for research? Revising drafts and editing pieces of writing? Staring out the window? Using the bathroom? Sharpening a pencil? Reading his independent reading book? (Circle all that apply.)

13. Does the student move on to other writing activities when the draft is finished? If not, what does this student choose to do?

**Figure 3.1** Engagement inventory from *A Closer Look*

interests can work on using those interests to improve students' attitudes. It's important to understand that students will have different needs. Their attitudes will improve with ownership of their workshop time. Students need to be able to move around the room to gather resources, find places to write comfortably, discuss their writing with others, and receive immediate (or close-to-immediate) feedback. They need to be able to have choices. We cannot forget to respect our writers and honor the work they do. Activities to build and maintain communities are rich and varied:

- Give out reading and writing inventories.
- Create surveys on readerly and writerly lives.
- Collect data to match up students for peer-response groups, realizing that they may not be perfect matches all the time; sometimes ask the kids who they work well with.

At the same time, it is necessary to examine our own attitudes toward writing and the teaching of writing. We may be a little scared, so what do we do? To begin with, you should know you are never alone in your classroom. There are great professional books out there (like the one you are reading!). A look at our reference list will help you start with a handful that will keep you going all year-round.

Then, there are the children's authors. Use your favorite authors' books as mentor texts, but remember to stay on top of new children's literature. You can follow people such as librarian John Schumacher (@MrSchuReads) and teacher Colby Sharp (@colbysharp) on Twitter to stay current with the latest Kidlit. Develop classroom sets of books by mentor authors, and encourage your students to find their own. Reread your mentor texts often. Stacey encourages teachers to balance the books they choose to use as mentor texts: "All students deserve to read mirror books, in which they see themselves, and window books, in which they learn about others (Bishop 1990). This means teachers must have books that represent a variety of religions, races, and sexual orientations in mentor-text baskets during all months of the year, not just in those with special designations such as Black History Month or Women's History Month" (Shubitz 2016, 5).

If you need help finding books that represent different groups, go to Social Justice Books' website (socialjusticebooks.org/booklists/), where you can find books categorized by holidays, ethnicity, race, and more.

To make work with mentor texts a little easier, Lynne often places sticky notes with ideas for minilessons on the inside end papers of each book for a quick reference. That way she can find the just-right book she needs when she confers with students or plans for instruction. When you make some notes, you will slow down and practice reading like a writer. This can help you gain confidence in your ability to teach the writers in your classroom. Never be afraid that you have a student or two who writes better than you do. It is quite possible, but that's a good thing! Each year you can learn from those students—new approaches, variations on a craft move, and more.

Share your thoughts and concerns with trusted others, but always look for ways you can learn more, problem solve, and turn a negative into a positive. If you are able, attend a course on writing from your closest National Writing Project site, or attend a state or national conference. There are plenty of Twitter chats (sites.google.com/site/twittereducationchats /education-chat-official-list) and blogs (such as *Two Writing Teachers*, and *Moving Writers*) to help you grow as a writer. Dive into the rich pool of knowledge that surrounds you. And find time to write yourself. Speaking of writing . . .

Social Justice Books

Twitter Education Chats

Two Writing Teachers

## *Teacher as Writer*

Perhaps most important of all, the idea of teacher as writer is an essential ingredient to success. In fact, Stacey regularly tells people that being a teacher who writes regularly is the secret to the success of a teacher of writers! A teacher participates as a member of the writing community by writing, often modeling during minilessons, writing in her writer's notebook and referring to it often, and sharing examples of the kinds of writing she does outside the classroom. When you share parts of a letter you are going to send to a friend, a card you created for a birthday, or a post on your blog, you are lifting the level of writing workshop by becoming

Moving Writers

another writer within the writing community. Teachers who do not write themselves only teach writing to students. Teachers who write teach writers, confer writer to writer (instead of teacher to student), and experience similar struggles with content choices, word choice, voice, organization, sentence fluency, and conventions. Teachers who write experience the joy of sharing their writing with others, too. It certainly would be difficult to teach someone how to play violin if you didn't play that instrument. We write to become more authentic teachers of writers, revealing our thoughts and interests to our students through our writing. We become more real to them when we are authors, too. Within a community of writers, teachers and students collaborate in a spirit of inquiry into their writing identities and writing processes. We start here with community to grow habits of mind, develop a growth mindset (Dweck 2007), gather knowledge about writing strategies to help them approach varying genres, and gain confidence in writing for pleasure and across many purposes.

Everywhere we travel, we hear similar stories from classroom teachers in grade levels from kindergarten to middle school. Lynne has kept a list from the many conferences she's attended. These comments were often spoken, varying slightly, but here is a "Top Ten" composite list from the last five years:

1. I never had a course on the teaching of writing, and I'm terrified to teach it!
2. I was never good at writing, and I'm scared of doing more harm than good.
3. Writing is hard, and most of my students don't like to write.
4. Writing takes more time than my schedule allows.
5. My students use language in their homes and neighborhoods that is different from the academic language we use in school. How does that affect writing instruction?
6. How can teachers who do not speak or understand a student's home language support them in their writing attempts?
7. We have so many curriculum demands . . . How can I give my students choice?

**A Principal Talks About Writing Community**

http://sten.pub/ww11

*Maggie Seidel, Principal*

8. I don't know where to begin. What skills and strategies should I teach with each unit of study? Is there a "right" way to approach this?

9. What mentor texts are appropriate for my grade level?

10. My district has a scripted program that I am required to use . . . so how do I have writing workshop?

Teacher as writer is an important concept for teachers. It helps us develop confidence and our skill set as writers. Through modeled and shared writing experiences, we can learn to enjoy writing and appreciate the hard work required to take a piece from the planning stages to publication. Dorfman and Cappelli (2017) ask teachers to write in front of their students as often as possible. They explain: "Like the hub of a giant wheel, it [the concept of teacher as writer] helps us connect the spokes of all our other teaching practices. In fact, teacher as writer is the core belief we must articulate to our students, our colleagues, and ourselves" (11). Students take in our process. They watch us get stuck, think, cross things out, add, and sometimes ask for their help. Thinking aloud while we write in front of our students models our process. Ralph Fletcher (2017a) lists these benefits of our writing in the classroom:

**The Many Reasons to Be a Teacher Who Writes**

http://sten.pub/ww12

*Melanie Meehan, Elementary Writing and Social Studies Coordinator*

- It will settle the class and set a serious tone.

- It's powerful modeling.

- It will encourage independence. If you're writing, it's less likely that they'll interrupt. This signals to students that they cannot always expect you to solve their problems.

- It will allow you to have authentic writing (yours) to share with the class.

- It lets you sample the vibe in the workshop. Is there a supportive environment, or are snarky comments commonplace? Writing and sharing your own writing is the best way to know for sure.

- Writing with your students builds sweat equity in the tone/ ambience of the workshop. Instead of saying, "I want you to be quiet," you earn the right to ask, "What kind of environment do we need so we can all do our best writing?"

Writing cannot be a spectator sport. It is important to play the game to improve. That includes teachers, too. As we write daily (for short bursts), we are learning to solve problems that arise. We try the craft moves and strategies we want our students to use and experiment with different forms and genres. The result: we become better at conferring with our student writers. It is easier to build a culture of trust when we are actively participating in our workshops by writing, too.

There are many ways to get started. Keep a notebook and try to write in it two or three times a week. Create entries that are sketches of characters (people in your life) and settings. Create lists such as "Things That Are Blue in June." Try some poetry; write down observations. Things are happening all around you. If you want some inspiration, join the Slice of Life Tuesdays hosted on the *Two Writing Teachers* blog. If you really want a challenge, join the monthlong Slice of Life Story Challenge, where you'll write every day in March and respond to at least three other bloggers. You will be amazed at the variety of topics and formats. Don't judge yourself—just write. Don't worry if some of your students share pieces that you think are better than yours. That happens all the time. Students will have more respect for you if you are a teacher of writers who writes. Their admiration and respect will increase every time you make the attempt and share.

## Writing Partnerships

We think it's important to implement writing partnerships during the first weeks of the school year. It doesn't matter if your students are new to one another or have known one another for years . . . Kids need help making good choices about whom they should choose as a writing partner (see Figure 3.2). (For instance, if your students have been with one another since kindergarten, they will likely partner up with their best friend if they're free to select whomever they want as a writing partner.) Therefore, we can help students make wise choices when it comes to whom they'll work with for a unit of study, a semester, or—if things go well—an entire school year!

A Mid-Workshop Conversation Between Writing Partners

http://sten.pub/ww13

*Missie Champagne, fourth-grade teacher*

**Figure 3.2** Students turn and talk with their writing partners.

It is important to have a conversation about what writing partners will do (e.g., provide honest feedback, assist with revision) and won't do (e.g., fix each other's spelling and grammar, take the pen and write for each other) when we're helping students think about whom they might want to partner up with. Depending on the size of your class, you might ask students to suggest three to four names of people with whom they would like to partner and one or two names of kids with whom they don't think they should work as a writing partner (see Figure 3.3). Typically, we tell students we will make every effort to match them with one of their requested partners. In addition, we guarantee students won't be matched—initially—with someone who is on their do-not-partner list.

## Teaching-Share

One of the greatest ways to build your community of writers is to showcase the work of all the writers in the classroom during the end-of-workshop share. This is a time to highlight the strategies students have tried in their

# Questionnaire

As you know, you will be required to work with other students throughout the course of the school year. You will have a partner for the following parts of the school day: read-aloud, reading workshop, and writing workshop. (You will also work with a partner AND a group during mathematics.) Therefore, think about the following questions CAREFULLY and then answer them in the space provided.

Name: _____ Date: _____

List the names of the four people you could work well with in a partnership:

1.

2.

3.

4.

List the name of the two people that you do NOT feel you can work with as a partner. (Tell me why you do not feel you can/should work with him/her.)

Student's Name: _____

Reason you cannot work with him/her:



Student's Name: _____

Reason you cannot work with him/her:

**Figure 3.3 Writing partner questionnaire** It is wise to ask students whom they think they can work well with in addition to whom they don't want to be paired with. Oftentimes, students ask not to be partnered with their best friend since they know they will socialize rather than do their work. In an effort to keep this from becoming a popularity contest, we ask students to complete questionnaires like this inside self-created study carrels made out of two-pocket folders. Once they are finished, no one sees the completed forms other than the classroom teacher.

writing. It's a time to showcase students' processes in ways that can be helpful for their classmates. Also, it's a time to share students' writing so students can see how their writing affects their classmates.

Leah Mermelstein (2007) suggests alternating between craft, content, process, and progress shares at the end of every writing workshop. Although each approach is different, all honor and reinforce writers' accomplishments by celebrating their work, positioning children as teachers, and nurturing the classroom writing community. It's important to track who has shared during the final five to ten minutes of writing workshop so every student's voice is heard. Too often, quiet kids won't raise their hand to share. In addition, striving writers may think they don't have anything to teach their peers if we don't nudge them toward sharing. It's important for every member of the class to understand that not only do they have something they can teach others how to do, but they can learn something about becoming a stronger writer from every member of the classroom community (see Figure 3.4).

# Celebrations

One of the easiest ways to infuse joy into your writing workshop is to celebrate the work of young writers. After all, we write to be read! Celebrations are a wonderful way to provide students with an audience while acknowledging their efforts so that they receive the fuel they need to keep writing.

Publishing parties are a traditional way to celebrate the work of young writers. At the end of a unit of study, you gather your students with their published pieces in hand, invite another class and their families, buy some treats, and celebrate. Although these end-of-unit celebrations are worthy of a class period, it is important to celebrate more often than at the end of each unit of study.

Not every celebration needs to include cake and juice. It's important to celebrate students throughout the writing process. Sometimes, you might want to celebrate with a high-five, a pat on the back, or a positive note home. These easy-to-do affirmations can occur at the end of the following:

- a coaching conference where the student took your guidance and moved forward on his own

| | |
|---|---|
| **Whole-Class Share** | Everyone gets a turn to share. This works well for a product share when the content will be only a few words, such as a title or a single line from a piece of writing. It helps to give the listeners an active role. The listeners can sit, notebooks in hand, ready to write down any tidbit they would like to use in future writing. |
| **Turn and Talk** | Talk to a partner. This is a nice alternative to the whole-class share. Everyone still gets a turn to share, but with a partner instead of the whole class. |
| **Anchor Chart** | Record the day's learning on a classroom chart. This is a concrete way to link back to the minilesson and reflect on the day's work. Rather than creating an anchor chart during the minilesson, save it for share time after students have had a chance to try their hand at the day's lesson. |
| **Thumbs Up/ Thumbs Down** | Restate the learning target for the day and have kids rate themselves as writers. For example, you could say, "Today we learned that writers sometimes use pictures to add detail to their writing. Think about yourself as a writer today. Thumbs up if your picture added detail, thumbs down if it didn't, and thumbs to the side if you're not sure." This only takes a minute to accomplish, but it encourages students to reflect on themselves as writers, and it gives you a quick reading of the class. |
| **Reflective Questions** | Ask students to think about themselves as writers. Examples: "What did you learn about yourself as a writer today?" "What did you try as a writer today?" "What did you struggle with as a writer today?" Everyone can share with a partner, a few students can share with the whole class, or everyone can simply sit quietly and think. |
| **Teacher Choice** | Strategically choose one or two students to share their process or product. Choose students who did an exemplary job of meeting the day's learning target or who took risks as writers. The students share their work or their thinking as writers, and share time becomes another opportunity to reinforce a teaching point. |
| **Written Response** | Instead of sharing orally, students can quickly reflect in writing on a sticky note or an exit ticket. This is helpful for the teacher who needs to do a whole-class assessment of the day's work or plan small-group work for the following day. |
| **Go Digital** | Use technology to share. Students can tweet out a reflection at the end of writing workshop or contribute to a class Google document. |

**Figure 3.4** Dana Murphy, a fifth-grade teacher and former literacy coach, compiled a list of share session possibilities for writing workshop, which she shared on the *Two Writing Teachers* website in 2014.

- trying a new strategy in the writer's notebook or an in-process piece of writing
- trying a craft move with a mentor text
- writing a draft where the writer took risks
- completing a strong flash draft
- thoughtful and/or substantial revisions
- editing a piece of writing for grammar, usage, mechanics, and spelling

Recognizing and noting students' accomplishments increases the number of positive interactions we have with students, which makes it possible for corrective actions to be taken well, since positive interactions help to develop and maintain trust (Aguilar 2017). We want students to listen when we speak, follow classroom rules, respect one another, and leave our classrooms as better writers. As a result, it is important to build a classroom community where we celebrate students' accomplishments—big and small—every day.

## Considerations for English Language Learners

As a workshop teacher, you will have to consider your use of resources and what can maximize instructional time for your English language learners. Mentor texts, particularly picture books, can help engage these students in risk taking. Allow students the freedom to sketch, use their own language, participate in oral rehearsal before they write, and partner with another writer to do some collaborative writing. Particularly helpful are metacognitive conversations where your writers stay for a one-on-one oral rehearsal of what they are going to write about before going back to their desk. These writers may stay on the rug where the community gathers and "practice" their thoughts with their teacher before engaging in independent writing time. Sometimes, we help these writers frame their thoughts by providing them with some suggestions and letting them choose.

## Final Thoughts

Elementary school classrooms provide the first opportunity for students to be part of a larger community and participate in democracy in action. Students learn how to have a conversation and respect their peers' opinions. Writing workshop prepares them to write arguments and deliberate in a civil fashion. As students participate in readerly and writerly conversations, establish ground rules for a respectful exchange of ideas. Remember, it is more than ensuring that students are treated fairly in the workshop environment and across the day; it is important for students to know that their community places a high value on fairness and equity (see Figures 3.5 and 3.6).

Sometimes, it may feel like we should plunge right in and not spend the time to get to know our students as writers, including their attitude toward writing, their successes, and their fears. Later on, we may realize this was a mistake. Building a community of writers in the beginning of the year will actually save time. We may spend time on finding the right writing partner or learning how to develop ways to contribute positively to writerly conversations. In writing workshop, we want to grow writers who are independent, who are willing to take risks, and who genuinely look forward to their time to write. As a teacher of writers who writes, you will grow these kinds of writers through a classroom culture that is inclusive, collaborative, joyful, and always moving writers toward greater independence.

## When You're Ready

Regie Routman (2018) urges educators to see their classroom day through their students' eyes. She asks us to "be sure the setting, tone, and classroom culture encourage and enhance risk taking, deep conversations, and meaningful learning" (52). She reminds us to make sure the students have ownership in the process of how the classroom is organized such as the library, publishing center, bulletin boards, and desks. Here, you have a chance to ask for your students' opinions and suggestions about what

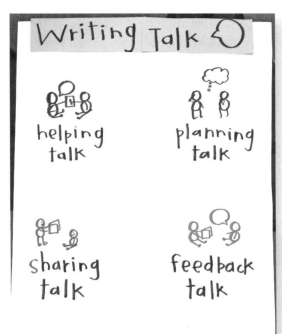

**Figure 3.5** Even our youngest writers can engage in different kinds of talk.

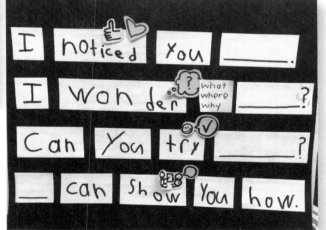

**Figure 3.6** Kindergartners learn how to ask respectful questions and offer thoughtful feedback.

is working and what needs some tweaking. You might create a survey for students that invites them to comment on room design, small-group design, classroom rules, discussion and publishing procedures, types of conferences, topic choice, and sense of belonging.

Students can use the survey, answers to which should remain anonymous, to let you know what's working for them. They can all relate to things such as the balance of power in the classroom. Where do they feel they have ownership? Other topics can relate to the general atmosphere—a sense of fairness, respect, and equity, understanding each other's needs. What about the pace of writing workshop? Too fast? Too slow? Just right?

For purposes of efficiency of the survey, allow students to respond to the questions and sections that speak to them instead of requiring that every student answer every question. Students can respond to areas they would like to discuss: workshop, opportunities for choice, thoughts about workshop priorities. (See the appendix for an example of such a survey.) Doing things like this throughout the year helps students understand that their voices are heard and their opinions count. Ownership in the intricate workings of writing workshop is important to the success of the community of writers.

# Chapter 4

# Classroom Management

## Practical Procedures and Predictable Routines

When we think back on the best teaching days of our lives, we often think of high-energy days when all of the students were engaged. We executed engaging lessons seamlessly. The kids "got it" and produced exquisite writing as a result of our teaching. Those perfect days were often few and far between during the first year each of us was a classroom teacher. Why? We didn't have our management down yet. Even if management is not your strength, it is never too late to improve!

To run an efficient writing workshop, it's crucial to move away from a "remind and punish" mindset toward "correct and teach" responses (Minor, 2019, 93); a classroom community where power is publicly shared (Ibid., 89). (See Chapter 3, "A Community of Writers.") Hertz and Mraz (2018) define management and community building this way:

CLASSROOM MANAGEMENT   A short-term control-based solution that often relies on punishments and rewards in lieu of teaching an alternate behavior.

COMMUNITY BUILDING   The thoughtful, long-term teaching, modeling, and habit-building of prosocial, positive behaviors (e.g., listening, resolving disputes with others, listening to others' points of view) and productive habits of mind (e.g., flexibility, resilience, empathy). (81)

As we mentioned in Chapter 3, our job as instructional leaders is to help students learn how to be part of a community of writers. When clear expectations are taught and discussed with students, children know what their role is in a minilesson, conference, and share session. If you take the first six weeks of school to teach students what you expect of them (and yourself!) during independent writing time, it becomes easier to provide highly individualized instruction, since your students know what their responsibilities are as writers. This is why we think it is important to take time to work diligently with your young writers during the first six weeks of school so your workshop runs efficiently for the duration of the school year.

Classroom management shouldn't be punitive. Rather, in this chapter you'll see a list of things we think you'll want to think about—before the school year begins—to help you solidify the procedures and routines you'll incorporate into your writing workshop. We think of procedures as how to do something, whereas routines are the day-to-day things students need to master so they can be independent.

## Procedures

Procedures are simply part of the routines that make writing workshop time rewarding and engaging for students. Procedures are what help students become more independent, especially if they are involved in the decision-making process for establishing those procedures. Teachers must plan ongoing structures that will support the work forever. Procedural structures will support the work all year long and should be created in the fall, even though they may not start right away.

- **Talk with students to create workshop expectations.** After several weeks of writing workshop, gather students on the rug and ask them to turn and talk about a set of writing workshop expectations (Shubitz 2016) they can agree on. Shubitz (2012) suggests asking students open-ended questions to start a discussion about workshop expectations, including the following:
  - ◆ Why should they write pieces that hold meaning or value to them?

♦ How can they use their voices to share ideas and opinions in a respectful way?

♦ How will they maintain their focus during independent writing time?

♦ What does accountable partner work look like?

♦ How should a productive and respectful share session look and sound?

Once you've created a list of expectations with students, post them on an anchor chart.

● **Teach students to come prepared for a minilesson:** It's crucial to maximize every instructional minute, so you will want students to be aware of what you want them to bring to the meeting area every day. Most of the time, you'll want students to bring a writing utensil and their writer's notebook and/or writing folder. You can make an announcement if you want them to bring additional items on a given day. Some teachers like to minimize the amount of verbal instructions they give students. If that's the case, you can have a space near your meeting area where you list the items they need to bring to the rug that day. Teach students to look at the list if you're going to refrain from giving verbal reminders.

● **Moving to and from the meeting area for a minilesson:** Whether you have a large or a small classroom, it's imperative to have kids come to the meeting area in an orderly fashion. The most efficient way to have kids move from their work spaces to the meeting area is to call tables or groups of kids to come at the same time. Another option is giving students two minutes to find the materials they need for the minilesson and walk to the meeting area, in a calm manner, after they push in their chairs. Lynne asks primary-grade students to move to and from the meeting area like "whispers." It always seems to work! Finally, you could use a rain stick to call students to the meeting area (Ayres and Shubitz 2010). Shaking a rain stick a few times provides students with a peaceful transition to get from their work spaces to the meeting area. If the flow to the

TWO WRITING TEACHERS

## How to Write a Plan for Independent Writing Time

HTTP://TWOWRITINGTEACHERS.ORG/2017/12/11/THEPLANBOX

### 1.) THINK ABOUT THE MINILESSON

Decide if the strategy you learned (today) could help you as a writer. If not, think about other strategies you've learned recently.

### 2.) THINK ABOUT THE WRITING PROCESS

Determine the kind of work you need to do based on where you are in the writing process.

### 3.) FILL YOUR TIME

Jot down what you will do first, second, third, etc. when you return to your focus spot.

### 4.) PLAN WISELY

Determine what you'll do if you finish early.

### 5.) SHARE YOUR PLAN

Have your teacher check your plan before leaving the meeting area. If necessary, revise your plan based on the feedback you receive.

**COMPILED BY STACEY SHUBITZ**

SOURCES:
1.) Day by Day: Refining Writing Workshop Through 180 Days of Reflective Practice (Stenhouse, 2010)
2.) https://twowritingteachers.org/?s=%22plan+boxes%22

**Figure 4.1** Making a plan for writing workshop

---

meeting area doesn't seem to be working, enlist the help of your students. It's possible they'll think of a different traffic pattern that will work better to get them to the meeting area safely.

When transitioning students from the meeting area to the places where they'll work during independent writing time, you may have students leave the rug with their writing partner or from the row in which they were sitting. If you check plan boxes (see more about them later in this chapter), then you'll dismiss students from the rug one by one after you have checked their plan for independent writing time (see Figure 4.1).

● **Model turning and talking with a partner during a minilesson.** Students should use six-inch voices so no one can hear what they are saying except their partner. They turn to face their partner and sit knee to knee. Partners should know who is Partner A and who is Partner B and take turns talking or sharing first, based on the teacher's instructions.

● **Teach students to request a conference.** There are many ways to do this. Students can sign up for a conference on a board that can be erased each day. The date is at the top of the board. When a student finishes her conference and is on her way back to her desk, she draws a line through her name and reads the next student's name so she can find that student and tap him or her on the shoulder. This process works well with intermediate grades. Younger students can pull a conference tent card (use brightly colored 5-by-8-inch index cards, laminated for durability year after year) and place them on their desks. The teacher can easily spot them and call those students for conferences.

- **Teach students to participate in conferences by coming prepared for a conference they request.** Students need to be the first reader of their work and to be able to ask questions for specific help. Chart some possible questions a writer might ask on a reread to do some revision and editing work and/or to prepare for a conference. Some questions might be, "Do I have a sharp focus, or do I need to remove some words, sentences, or even paragraphs?" "Would dialogue help give voice to my narrative?" "Did I vary my sentence length to make my piece more interesting and readable?"

- **Model effective conferences by using your own writing.** Invite another teacher and student to give you feedback for your question(s) while the class listens. You can sit in the center, and your class can gather around you in a circle (the fishbowl technique). They can write a suggestion to share on a sticky note, too. Prepare questions or statements that help your student peer responders give you specific suggestions. Prepare some simple checklists that students can use to examine their own writing. Share questions for each type of writing that may help students either problem solve before the conference or know where the piece needs some work. For more questions, see page 87 in *A Closer Look: Learning More About Our Writers with Formative Assessment* (Dorfman and Dougherty 2017).

## NARRATIVE

Is your story about one thing? Is there a place for a splash of dialogue? What is the problem in your story? Does your story have a satisfying ending?

## INFORMATIONAL

What is your text about? What made you choose this topic? Did you present the information in a logical order? How did you develop your ideas? With anecdotes? Statistics? Experts' quotes?

## OPINION

What made you choose this topic and position? What is your most important evidence to support your opinion? What kind of tone (expert? angry? whiny?) does your piece have? What makes you think so?

Students can use these questions to confer with the teacher on her own writing. This will help them internalize questions for a self-conference.

- **Choose publishing methods that work for your classroom.** After the final editing conference, students can have options. Perhaps they can "publish" their work by using a laptop. Sometimes, publishing includes artwork. In Lynne's fourth-grade classroom, students created black-and-white ink drawings using pens and paintbrushes of various thicknesses for their haiku. In Shelly Keller's kindergarten classroom, students created a cover page and added illustrations for their books. The students could choose the paper size from the publishing center. When they were ready for a final conference, they placed a paper clip on their pages and placed their book in a bin on Shelly's desk. When they held their final conference, Shelly stapled their book together for them. These books were shared with partners, the whole group, and parents. Kindergarten students "published" book recommendations in a colorful flyer that their teacher created to help parents and their children with summer reading. In Stacey's upper-elementary classrooms, students stapled all their drafts into a manila folder beneath their final published piece. Then, each student used the artistic medium of their choosing to design a cover for their published piece. Regardless of the grade, it is important to have opportunities throughout the year to do something extraordinary to celebrate students' published writing.

Creating effective procedures will help students gain confidence in their ability to operate independently of the teacher. For a smoothly running workshop, teachers must plan ongoing structures that will support the work forever. Of course, they can be modified from year to year.

Procedural structures support work all year long, but not all procedures may be used in the first several weeks (such as how to publish a book or how to have a peer conference). Posting rules for everyone to see and visit on their own to clear up confusion is essential: post center procedures, conference rules and procedures, publishing guides, and discussion guidelines where students can easily refer to them so you don't have to stop to explain them. Use pictures and photos to help younger students "read" the rules and guidelines. Practical procedures save time for both teacher and student!

## Routines

In the beginning of the year, a teacher establishes the routines for various components of workshop. Students will need to know how to use the writing center, when and how to ask to use the bathroom, when pencil sharpening is permitted, how to sign up for a conference, how to turn in work, when and how to share their writing, and so on.

It is important to have several routines in place so you'll be able to hold successful, uninterrupted conferences. Therefore, one of the first things you'll need to do is make sure the students who are not having a conference with you are continuing to use their time productively. Echoes of "I'm finished!" can be eliminated if students know what options exist. In late September, we can begin by creating an anchor chart called "What I Can Do During Writing Workshop." For an example of an anchor chart from Karen Rhoads's fourth-grade classroom, see Figure 4.2.

## Eliminating Distractions

Every writer works differently. Stacey is the kind of writer who needs total silence when she's in the writing zone, whereas Lynne can write with the television on, Welsh corgis barking, and people having a conversation all around her. In fact, Lynne does better with some noise—such as music playing in the background—than she does with total silence. Everyone is different. The truth is, most of our students could accomplish more with fewer distractions. We've come up with some ideas for reducing

# What I Can Do
# During Writing Workshop

◆ Read my notebook entries

◆ Research a writing topic

◆ Find a topic by using my heart map, hand map, or memory chain

◆ Create a neighborhood map

◆ Make lists (strong verbs, favorite leads, quiet and noisy words)

◆ Revising and editing

◆ Creating a dedication page

◆ Creating a cover page

◆ Participate in a peer conference

◆ Hold a self-conference

◆ Begin a new writing piece

◆ Revise a published piece by writing it in a different format

◆ Study a mentor text to imitate a craft move

◆ Study a mentor author to imitate his/her craft moves

**Figure 4.2** What I can do during workshop

distractions during writing workshop, since we think it's important to maximize writing time by having as few interruptions as possible.

- Moving chairs around the classroom: It might sound like a no-brainer, but students should practice moving chairs around the classroom in ways that will not distract other students. Whether students are moving their desk chair to work with you in a small group or to sit beside their writing partner for a peer conference, they should practice using two hands, with the chair legs a few inches off the floor so that everyone is safe.

- Bathroom/water break: Most teachers do not allow students to leave the classroom during minilessons unless it's an emergency. Although we want kids working during independent writing time, it is often necessary for students to use the bathroom. To eliminate disruptions, it is useful to teach them basic sign language (i.e., the signs for *toilet*, *yes*, and *no*) so they can ask permission to use the bathroom without saying a word if you're conferring with a student or working with a small group. Once the student catches your eyes, you can simply tell them yes or no with the movement of your hand.

Other teachers choose to eliminate themselves completely from the bathroom sign-out process by allowing students to sign out a bathroom pass if one is available at the time the child needs to leave the room. Tech-savvy teachers might have students use the classroom iPad to scan a QR code when they depart to and return from the bathroom.

In terms of trips to the water fountain, the best way to eliminate the need for students to leave the room is to allow each student to keep a water bottle on their desk that they are in charge of filling each morning.

### Writing Utensils

- Pens versus pencils (and when to use the sharpener): Pencils can be sharpened at the beginning of the day. Additional pencils can be placed in small trays or cups on every table or placed in the supply section of the classroom. However, you may want to consider using pens—at any grade level. We suggest this because erasing slows down the writing process and often results in smudges and/or tears.

Determine whether pens or pencils are best for your writing workshop.

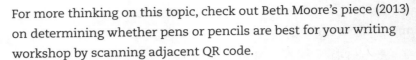

For more thinking on this topic, check out Beth Moore's piece (2013) on determining whether pens or pencils are best for your writing workshop by scanning adjacent QR code.

- Colored pens are useful for revisions and edits. Students can easily track the changes they've made as they produce multiple drafts. It's also easy for you to see the tracks of your teaching—the craft moves from minilessons—right there in the revisions and edits.

## Using Paper

In many elementary school classrooms, students draw and write on paper. Some important procedures will help students keep track of their work and help them with drafting issues. Nothing is worse for a young child learning how to hold a pencil and write (print) using upper- and lowercase letters and spacing as well as trying to use lined paper than having to copy his entire writing piece over to do any revision work. Here are some ideas to help students keep track of their pieces, cut down on the need to recopy entire pieces multiple times, and be able to reread their work to revise and edit. In addition, we make sure students have easy access to paper, while teaching them how to take only what they need so they don't waste classroom resources. These tips can help you manage the paper chase.

- Match students with paper choices that align to their stage of writing development. All kids need paper that meets them where they're at while pushing them just a bit further. Beth Moore defines the stages of writing as early emergent writers (pre-k and kindergarten), emergent writers (kindergarten and first grade), beginning writers (kindergarten–second grade), transitional writers (first–third grades), intermediate writers (second–fourth grades), advanced intermediate writers (third grade and beyond), fluent writers (third grade and beyond), and advanced fluent writers (fourth grade and beyond).

  - For an infographic about paper choice explore Beth Moore's piece on the stages of writing development. Scan QR code and scroll down until you reach the infographic.

Paper choice infographic

Downloadable
paper choices

- ◆ For a variety of free paper choices you can download, scan QR code and check out Beth Moore's website.

- Have students write their name and date on papers (just the date in their notebooks). Students should date all entries in a journal or notebook as well as loose papers used for drafting. They should place their name in the same location each time for identification purposes. Teach students to choose paper that will show off their writing and/or drawing and is an appropriate size for their handwriting.

- Have students skip every other line so they can revise their work without recopying everything. Skipping lines makes it easier to read student writing as well. Often, the students find it easier to make an "X" in the margin of the lined paper for every other line so they remember to only write on those lines. Eventually, it will become automatic. In a writer's notebook, skipping every other line is not required.

- Having students write on one side of their paper helps them look at their work as a whole (they can lay sheets side by side). It is especially important when including illustrations, or using features of nonfiction writing. Layout becomes even more important when we write the final draft on computers.

- Encourage students to use legible but not perfect handwriting. Perfect handwriting will slow writers down to the point where they may lose an idea (their brains are operating faster than their hands can write!). However, they must be able to reread their work to confer with the teacher or a peer or even to revise and edit over the course of several days.

## Communal Supplies

Students should also have easy access to writing materials (paper, markers, colored pencils, glue sticks, sticky notes) so they are not asking you for these items while you are trying to confer. Ayres and Shubitz (2010) suggest keeping caddies or containers at the center of a cluster of desks that contain a variety of writing implements. They suggest doing several procedural minilessons for using and taking care of all classroom supplies so they last from September to June.

Reference materials such as dictionaries, thesauruses, rhyming dictionaries, and atlases are helpful and should be accessible to students, too.

## Turning in Work

Systems are important when collecting student work so the paper chase doesn't get the best of you. Here are a few things to consider when developing systems for having students hand in their work.

- Work in progress: As students are drafting, revising, and editing their writing, you'll want to check in to see how things are going. Although you might not have time to read every draft every student writes, you should certainly collect all of your students' drafts and read at least one from each student during each unit of study. Reading through students' in-process writing will help you identify small groups who might benefit from doing some work with you, conferences you need to have with a given student, or full-class minilessons you will want to teach.

- Writer's notebooks checking days: Some teachers peruse their students' writer's notebooks during a writing conference. However, if you're keeping each writing conference to about five minutes, that doesn't give you enough time to read students' notebooks closely to see how they're making use of the strategies you're teaching. If you want to *really* get a feel for how students are working in their writer's notebooks, it is useful to read each student's notebook once a week. Take the total number of students in your class and divide by five so you have a handful of writer's notebooks to read through each day. Provide students with reminders to turn in their writer's notebook to a particular place on their notebook-checking day so you can read it during part of your lunchtime or during a preparation period when the students are out of the classroom.

# Planning

Although planning (or prewriting) can be accomplished in many ways, it is crucial to the process. When students learn how to plan, they can use their independent writing time more efficiently and effectively. As you do a quick check with students, their plans often reveal whether they are ready to write or need more support. You will need to model how to plan multiple times in the beginning of the year and perhaps again as you introduce new genres and formats for writing.

- How do I use my independent writing time (primary)? Students in every grade often indicate where they are in the process through a status-of-the-class check. The teacher asks each student to tell her whether they are planning, researching, drafting, revising, in need of a conference, or ready to publish. This simple check-in takes about two to three minutes. Often, teachers circulate during independent writing time to hold conferences or give gentle nudges to students who are stuck. Students know that this time is for writing, drawing, and holding a self-conference to make some revisions, even before a teacher conference.

- Plan boxes (upper elementary). "Plan boxes are tools that help students self-manage their independent writing time" (Ayres and Shubitz 2010, 17). Students' plans should be checked at the end of a minilesson to help you determine their intentions for their independent writing time. A well-written plan is like a to-do list that can help a child stay focused during independent writing time (see Figures 4.3 and 4.4). In addition, reading over them can help you determine who needs a writing conference with you. You may be able to determine who needs your time by noticing things that seem challenging for a student, or a student might directly request a conference with you when she writes her plan.

**Figure 4.3** A teacher showcases one of her student's plan boxes under the document camera.

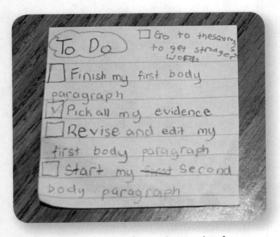

**Figure 4.4** Sample of a student's plan for independent writing time

## Status of the Class

Nancie Atwell (1998) introduced the concept of "status of the class." This valuable tool helps student writers and their teachers set goals and monitor progress. Status of the class tracks where students are in the process and helps them recognize that they are being held accountable for the work that they do daily. We cannot meet with every student every day or sometimes even every week, but taking a status of the class each day at the beginning of writing workshop is a way to keep track of progress on a weekly basis. Through this three-minute routine at the end of the minilesson, we can determine which students need our immediate attention, which students might just need a conference, and which students are okay working independently that day (Dorfman and Dougherty 2017). Knowing where your student writers are in the process is important. The teacher does a roll call and students respond with one of the following answers: Planning, Drafting, Revising, Editing, Publishing, Need a Conference. Sometimes a teacher includes Researching. If a student has been planning for several days without moving forward, we need to know why. Is it because the writer is having trouble finding an appropriate topic? Or is he having difficulty with an organizational format for his writing piece? Conferring with this student will clear this up. Not all students ask for a conference before they have completed a draft, so keeping tabs on the status of the class would alert us to the need for a conference for this student. If you keep a folder on your computer for status of the class, you can project it onto a screen to help students pair with each other for a peer conference. For example, if you are waiting for a conference, you could decide to share your piece of writing with another student who is also waiting for a conference.

Sometimes, a teacher will choose to conduct a status of the class at the end of writing workshop. This practice can help the teacher get ready for the next day by organizing previous conference notes and what student(s) could benefit from such as a lesson on drafting, revising, or editing. This activity helps teachers track their students' writing habits and holds students accountable to use workshop time for writing purposes. During status of the class, the teacher can offer positive reinforcement for students who have finished drafts and revisions, or who are ready to publish or start something new. Gentle nudges to stay focused and engaged can be offered, too, if the teacher notices a student(s) is moving very slowly through a piece of writing. Every so often, a teacher can administer status of the class both after the minilesson time and again at the end of workshop to informally assess how much students have been able to accomplish during independent writing time.

**Status of the Class**

http://sten.pub/ww14

*Kelly Gallagher,
second-grade teacher*

## Final Thoughts

We know it's tempting to dive into your first unit of study at the start of the school year. However, taking the time to teach routines and procedures during the first six weeks will pay dividends throughout the year. Because students will have had time to practice every routine and procedure during the first few weeks, it will take only a quick reminder to get them back on track when things go awry later.

That being said, don't be afraid to take the time to teach into management-related things during the school year. Sometimes the anticipation of a special event or the days after a school vacation can lead to students forgetting basic classroom expectations. Take a few minutes to discuss your concerns with your students. Practice the routine or procedure they're forgetting with them until it is done properly. From there, it should be smooth sailing!

## When You're Ready

When students collaborate to do group work—research for a project or presentation, writing an opinion piece, creating a science fiction story, developing a fifth-grade survival guide—they will be more committed to the work if they can manage their expectations and time. You may want to provide some exemplars for group contract work and even suggest that they create one that will fit their expectations for a particular project. Here is an example:

- We will use our computer time to focus on research needed for our project.
- We will check in with group members if we are absent from school.
- We will hold each other accountable.
- We will treat each other fairly and with respect.
- We will make sure all group members have a voice in the work to complete the project.

Encourage students to sign off on these agreements, and let them come up with a logical consequence for violating them. This will empower students to take accountability into their own hands and manage themselves. Students are more responsible when they can take part in the management of their time, resources, and responsibilities.

# Chapter 5

# Whole-Class Instruction

## Setting a Positive Tone and Building Enthusiasm

The whole-group setting is where teachers can set a positive tone by gathering the writing community for instruction. Here, we move students to independence by offering instruction through demonstration and guided practice. We share a mentor text, we present a piece of high-quality literature as an exemplar, and we model with our own writing. Our goal is to move students to independent practice as soon as possible so that the students are in charge, making decisions and self-regulating most of their work in writing workshop.

Of course, it takes a lot of work to feel comfortable with choosing a mentor text and modeling with your own writing. Moving from modeling to active engagement and then to independent writing and reflection takes practice and refinement. Planning helps. Being a writer and taking time to write something in your notebook as often as possible will start to feel natural, and you'll grow in confidence and expertise. Give yourself a year or two to wade into the workshop waters, splash around a bit, and swim in the shallow part of the pool. You will soon be ready to cannonball off the diving board! If we provide the right mentor text, share our own writing to teach a strategy, or use student writing that demonstrates our teaching point, then most of our students can successfully self-monitor as they write independently with little support from the teacher. Just give it time. You and your students will grow together as a writing community.

## Minilessons: The Basics

Minilessons are short, explicit lessons taught at the beginning of a writing workshop session to help students learn the essential elements of writing. Minilessons are five to fifteen minutes long and provide the opportunity to teach students one new strategy while giving them some time to practice what's been taught before the independent writing portion of writing workshop. Lucy Calkins (1994) describes minilessons this way:

> The minilesson is our forum for making a suggestion to the whole class—raising a concern, exploring an issue, modeling a technique, reinforcing a strategy. Although minilessons may often look like miniature speeches, like brief lectures, they are entirely different from the lectures that were such a part of my own schooling. The difference can be summed up in a single word: context. In minilessons, we teach into our students' intentions. Our students are first deeply engaged in their self-sponsored work, and then we bring them together to learn what they need to know in order to do that work. This way, they stand a chance of being active meaning-makers, even during this bit of formal instruction. First our students are engaged in their own important work. Then we ask ourselves, "What is the one thing I can suggest or demonstrate that might help the most?" (193–194)

Minilessons come from many places. Many people use local or national standards to help them decide what to teach students. Other people use the scope and sequence provided by a district-purchased curriculum, such as the Teachers College Reading and Writing Project's *Units of Study*, to help them determine what minilessons to teach. However, minilessons should also come from what you're noticing in your classroom with your students.

Therefore, you might teach a minilesson that is the outgrowth of a one-on-one conference, from reading student writing, or from a reflection you or a student has done about writing (see Figure 5.1). In other words, being a responsive teacher is a great way to find things to teach students during the whole-class instructional time.

| Teacher's Role During a Minilesson | Students' Role During a Minilesson |
|---|---|
| • Connect to students' prior knowledge.<br>• Provide explicit instruction on one strategy.<br>• Call on students to share out something they tried during active engagement.<br>• Link the teaching point to the work students will do when they return to their seats. | • Come prepared with materials . . . or with nothing at all.<br>• Sit with your talking (writing) partner.<br>• If your writing partner isn't present, sit near another partnership so you have someone to talk to when necessary.<br>• Keep hands free of writing utensils when the teacher is teaching.<br>• Communicate using nonverbal gestures when asked.<br>• Raise your hand and wait to be called on if your teacher asks for volunteers.<br>• Stay on-topic when you turn and talk with your writing partner.<br>• Make a plan, based on what your teacher says, for how your independent writing time will go. |

**Figure 5.1** Keep your minilessons from turning into maxilessons by having minilesson expectations. Here are some typical things we expect teachers and kids to do during a minilesson.

The Four
Components of a
Minilesson

http://sten.pub/ww15

*Melanie Meehan,
Elementary Writing
and Social Studies
Coordinator*

A Minilesson
to Foster
Independence

http://sten.pub/ww16

*Missie Champagne,
fourth-grade teacher*

# Architecture of a Minilesson

Regardless of the content (whether you're teaching a collecting strategy, demonstrating with a mentor text, or dealing with a procedure for publishing a piece at the end of a unit of study), it's important to follow the basic architecture—connection, teaching, active engagement, and a link—of a minilesson. This predictable format is useful for students because it allows you to activate their prior knowledge, teach them something, give them a chance to try it, and then connect it to the work they're doing as writers. Here are some basics to keep in mind for each part of the minilesson:

**Connection** Start by connecting to the writers' prior knowledge. You'll want to show enthusiasm so you inspire and invigorate students to pay attention to your teaching. You might want to talk about how the lesson you're about to teach fits with the work they've already done as writers and how it will fit into their lives as writers. During the connection, you might involve students in a small way by reminding them of what they already know. You might encourage participation by having students answer a couple of your questions with a thumbs-up or thumbs-down or by having a *brief* turn and talk with a writing partner. This small amount of participation will engage students and add a bit of socialness to the lesson without throwing open the door for everyone to comment (which would turn your minilesson into a maxilesson!). Finally, you'll name your teaching point.

Phrases to use in the Connection part of your minilesson include these:

- "Yesterday we were working on . . ."
- "Today I want to teach you . . ." (name your teaching point)
- "In our mentor text, the author . . ." (name the author's craft)

**Teach** Next you will teach your students a new strategy you want them to use as writers, not just that day but for the rest of their lives. You might demonstrate by using a published mentor text, a text written by a student, or something you've written yourself. Students should be able to see the purpose of what you teach when they're watching you teach.

**Figure 5.2** The teacher engages students during the minilesson by using her own writing as a demonstration text.

These phrases will help you frame the Teach part of your minilesson:

- "When I write . . ."
- "Watch me as I show you how I . . ." (set up demonstration)
- "Did you notice how I . . ."
- "When authors write . . ."
- "Let's study this text together . . ." (set up demonstration)
- "Did you notice how the author . . ."

**Active Engagement**  You'll provide students with a chance to have a go with what was taught in the demonstration. Students will try the strategy independently or with their writing partner. As the teacher, you'll walk around the meeting area to observe and support students as they try what was taught. Be sure the active engagement you select matches the teaching you did earlier in the minilesson.

Phrases to help you set up the Active Engagement and debrief it include these:

- "Now it is your turn to try it."
- "You (and your partner) are going to . . ."
- "I noticed . . ."

**Link** You'll bring closure to the minilesson by linking back to what the class already knows about writing, what was taught during the lesson, and how they can use the strategy *today and every day* as writers (see Figure 5.3). You'll end with giving students a charge by saying something like, "I'd like everyone to try this strategy in their writing today" or "You can put this strategy into your toolbox of writing strategies. Pull it out anytime you want to . . ."

Phrases to use in the Link include these:

- "Today and every day, I want you to remember that writers . . ."

## Minilesson Checklist

- All students were engaged in the connection. (YES NO)
- The teaching point was clear by the end of the connection. (YES NO)
- The teacher set up the demonstration explicitly so students knew what they were watching, what they should be looking for, and/or what they should do. (YES NO)
- The demonstration reflected the teaching point stated in the connection. (YES NO)
- The teacher recapped the demonstration. (YES NO)
- The teacher restated the teaching point after recapping the demonstration. (YES NO)
- The teacher set up the active engagement. (YES NO)
- All students were involved in the active engagement. (YES NO)
- The active engagement matched the demonstration. (YES NO)
- The teacher brought closure to the active engagement by sharing what she or he noticed and/or by highlighting a couple of students. (YES NO)
- The link restated the teaching point in the same language used at the end of the connection. (YES NO)
- The link gave the students direction, rather than an assignment, for what to do next. (YES NO)

*Adapted from Upper Grade Summer Institute Writing Packet (2005, 36).*

**Figure 5.3 Minilesson Checklist** Use this checklist to determine whether your minilesson has all its components.

# *Types of Minilessons*

You can use the minilesson architecture as the bones of any type of mini-lesson you wish to teach. However, it's important to note there are four different ways you might engage your students when teaching them a new strategy (see Figure 5.4).

> ## Four Types of Teaching
>
> - **Demonstration** The teacher shows students how to use a strategy to improve their writing in a step-by-step manner.
>
> - **Guided Practice** The teacher coaches the students through the strategy using lean prompts.
>
> - **Explanation with Example** The teacher provides students with an example of the strategy and provides an explanation with how to carry out that strategy in their own writing.
>
> - **Inquiry** The teacher invites students to study with her, which enables the students to discover something new, name what they're noticing, and transfer it to their own writing.

**Figure 5.4** There are four teaching methods we commonly use.

Teachers College Reading and Writing Project recommends four types of instruction for writing workshop: demonstration, guided practice, expla-nation with example, and inquiry (Calkins, Hohne, and Robb, 2015, 71–73). Lucy Calkins (2013) likens the four methods of teaching writing to the way adults teach young children how to put on their shoes.

- Demonstration: The more knowledgeable party includes a narration to guide the person putting on the shoe with a step-by-step process.

Students' Takeaways from a Minilesson

http://sten.pub/ww17

Melanie Meehan, Elementary Writing and Social Studies Coordinator

- Guided Practice: An adult helps a child go through the process of putting on shoes while also providing directions for what to do with each foot and each shoe as they go along.

- Explanation with Example: The adult might give the child a lecture about how to put on the shoe by telling and possibly showing the child how to do it. He might share some tips along the way, but overall, the adult must do a lot of prep work to make sure the verbal explanation and visual examples of putting on shoes make sense.

- Inquiry: The adult might ask the child to figure out how the shoe got on his foot. The adult would ask questions to engage the child until the child could accurately explain how he got the shoe on his foot (Shubitz 2016).

# Things You Can Teach in Minilessons

## PROCEDURES

Minilessons are versatile and can be used to accomplish many things. In the beginning of the year, they are often procedural. For example, a simple mini-lesson might demonstrate how students use the classroom library. There may be a special shelf for mentor texts that students return to on their own. Each teacher may have a method for signing out a book and a time limit for keeping it. In Bruce Bloome's fourth-grade classroom, class sets of Ralph Fletcher's *A Writer's Notebook*, *Poetry Matters*, and *Live Writing* were stored in bins for easy access. A small notebook was also stored for students to sign and date when they borrowed a book and when they returned it. Bruce occasionally reminded the students to return a book they were not reading or using.

## MANAGEMENT

Time is the currency of education. It is important to find ways to make every minute count. Management issues can cut into valuable instructional time. One way to save time is to assign "talking partners" or "elbow partners" in elementary grades. When children are gathered as a whole community on a rug or in one designated area in the classroom, the expectation is that there will be time to turn and talk. Assigning partners and modeling for children what they should do if their partner is not present will save lots of time.

Other management minilessons include where students can sit to draft or confer; where to store notebooks, works in progress, and finished drafts; and when to take bathroom trips and sharpen pencils. Brenda Krupp's third-grade class held a meeting to discuss how they could manage the classroom talk and the need for silence during writing workshop. The students worked in small groups to investigate locations in the classroom where talk was more appropriate. Lynne suggested a banner might be posted for the first ten minutes of independent writing time—"Shhhh! Everybody's writing!"—so students would know that during this time, no one was conferring with a partner or the teacher, pencils were not to be sharpened, and trips to the bathroom were allowed on an emergency basis only. The students listed their ideas on an anchor chart, and a classroom map with quiet zones was posted.

## WRITING PROCESS

A solid understanding of your own writing process will help you teach students how to think about their process. Part of your instruction can be spent having conversations about stages of the writing process: planning, drafting, revising, editing, and publishing. A caution here is to remember that writing processes are recursive in nature, not linear.

- **Planning or Prewriting**

Brainstorm and write down everything you can think of that might relate to the topic, and then reread and evaluate the ideas you generated. It's easier to cut out bad ideas than to think of only good ones. Once you have a handful of useful ways to approach your topic, you can make a list, create a web or drawing, talk with a partner, or just start writing. Remember to be flexible; this is just a way to get you writing. If better ideas occur to you as you're writing, don't be afraid to refine your original ideas.

● **Drafting**

After you have written down your ideas with the help of one or more prewriting strategies, start writing. Some writers like to edit as they move through a draft; others like to pour out their thoughts on paper. Reread both silently and aloud, and read for sensibility.

● **Revise**

Improve what the piece says and how it says it by adding description, imagery, and details. Take out unnecessary words and phrases. Use peer suggestions to improve. Clarify by adding examples, anecdotes, and/or explanations. Make sure your piece has voice! Make every word count. Strong verbs and exact nouns are important here.

● **Editing**

Work on editing for mechanics and spelling. Take your time and edit for one thing at a time. Reread only for capitalization. Read again for punctuation, and a third time for spelling. Dictionaries and environmental print can be used here! Students will write one final draft after edits are completed. This will often involve the teacher as final editor, especially if the work is going to be read by audiences other than the teacher. It is good to remember that the writer should always be the first reader of her work at every stage of the writing process. Editing should be the job of the writer. However, the teacher is the final copyeditor. Peers are great for offering revision tips but not particularly for editing.

● **Publishing**

Students publish their written pieces, sending their work to publishers, reading their finished stories aloud, making books. This is a time for celebration!

Writers need to understand the writing process, and teachers need to model all aspects of it for them. Students are regularly reminded of the importance of process and sometimes discuss their process during share sessions. Teachers explicitly teach and model revision and editing strategies.

# Using Mentor Texts

A mentor text is a piece of writing, often a picture or chapter book, that can be used many times throughout the school year to encourage students to take risks and try new things. In *Craft Moves*, Shubitz (2016) tells us, "Teachers use mentor texts to teach students how to lift the level of their writing" (3). Since mentor texts are often first used as a read-aloud and returned to several times to highlight an organizational structure, a sentence pattern, punctuation, or a craft move, they become familiar, and students are comfortable imitating them. Dorfman and Cappelli (2017) say that mentor texts help students move beyond their comfort zones—to take risks and stretch outside their "writing box"—and inspire student writers to reinvent themselves as writers, growing and changing in skill set, sophistication, and, we would add, in imagination.

Designating a special location for the mentor texts you will use in a year is a good idea. You will use mentor texts in some minilessons as the literature hook in Your Turn lessons (see later in chapter), in individual and small-group conferences, and in whole-group final reflection and sharing. Sometimes, you will ask students to examine books written by a mentor author to study a craft move or use a strategy. For example, if you are looking at leads, you may look at a set of Patricia Polacco books to notice attention to setting and character snapshots. Sometimes all you need to do is pull a book and say to a student who is struggling with closure for a narrative, "Let's look at what Don Crews did in *Shortcut*. Remember what happened in the story? Yes, that's right. He wanted to teach his readers a lesson and let us know what his characters were thinking and feeling long after the event was over. Would those strategies fit your story?" Sometimes, several mentor texts can be mentioned in a short minilesson, almost as a gentle reminder, before independent writing. If your students, for example, are working on creating a fitting title for their piece, you may simply display a few mentor texts on a document imager and remind students to capitalize all the important words in a title—and always the first and last words. This may be enough for a particular writing session. However, sometimes you need a longer lesson, especially when you are introducing something new and important.

# The Your Turn Lesson

In *Writing Essentials: Raising Expectations and Results While Simplifying Teaching* (2005), Regie Routman discusses an Optimal Learning Model that thrives in a social environment where students are encouraged to collaborate, confer, take risks, and transfer learning from the minilesson to their actual writing. In this model, Routman suggests we move our writers through a process of demonstration and shared demonstration to guided practice and independent practice. Through this model, teachers gradually release responsibility to their students.

Although modeling is a fairly common practice among elementary school teachers, shared and guided practice is often missing. Routman says most of her teaching is accomplished through shared writing experiences and scaffolded conversations. She goes on to explain that guided writing occurs during whole-group instruction. Here writers try to apply what has been demonstrated by the teacher and often practiced again during shared writing, often with a partner or small group. The teacher can support this work through roving conferences and whole-group shares during reflection time. Of course, the goal is to get students to try new strategies and craft moves in their independent writing. The teacher hopes to see the tracks of her teaching in the independent writing pieces her students produce.

Dorfman and Cappelli (2017) describe a lesson format they have called the "Your Turn lesson" that is not specific to any grade level or classroom and also follows the gradual release of responsibility model put forth by Lev Vygotsky. The sequence of instruction moves methodically and meaningfully from teacher control to student independence. This model suggests that cognitive work should move slowly and intentionally from teacher modeling to shared responsibility between teachers and students to independent practice and application by the learner (Pearson and Gallagher 1983). Pearson and Gallagher explain that the critical stage of the model is the guided practice (the active engagement in Calkins's minilesson design). This is the stage at which the teacher gradually releases task responsibility to the students. Sometimes, guided practice may be extended for students who need another go or simply need to remain on the rug and have a conversation with the teacher and/or peers to feel ready to write independently.

In her groundbreaking book *Reading To, With, and By Children* (1990), New Zealand educator Margaret Mooney introduced teachers to the stages of reading development and the teaching approaches of shared, guided, and independent reading. Mooney talked about the I Do, We Do, You Do model of instruction. This model, applied to writing workshop, basically looks like this:

**I Do** Tell students what they need to know, and model for them how to do the things they need to be able to do. Research confirms this is an essential component of an effective and efficient learning process. This is where you, as the teacher, have control and can involve many strategies, including informing, explaining, modeling with your writing, and providing examples from the literature and student samples.

**WE Do** Often as a whole group at first, and then in small groups as needed, we work together. In writing workshop, creating a shared writing experience you can return to for revision and editing work is often the key to students' future success.

**YOU Do** Here, student writers independently practice what you have already taught them. Practicing within the context of their own drafts will help students retain the new strategy or craft move and become fluent with what they must be able to do. It is important to see the tracks of your teaching in your students' writing. If they are not trying it independently, they most probably will not remember it or apply it in future writing. Of course, it is important you offer feedback along the way through one-on-one conferences and end-of-workshop whole-group reflection.

A gradual release model allows teachers to engage with students effectively because students become proficient with essential components of writing workshop. The gradual release provides demonstration—teachers modeling (writing) in front of their students—to immerse writers in new concepts before they approximate the learning. This lesson design then establishes a clear sense of ownership as students write independently and share their thinking with others in the final reflection. Throughout the gradual release, a variety of voices are heard for discussing new learning in kid-friendly talk that makes use of the nomenclature of writers.

## Writing Your Own Teaching Points

There will be many times when you want to teach your students a strategy to help them become stronger writers. As a result, you will need to write your own minilesson. You'll want to use the minilesson architecture we shared earlier in the chapter to help you frame your lesson. However, before you write the lesson, you will need to craft a well-written teaching point.

In *DIY Literacy: Teaching Tools for Differentiation, Rigor, and Independence* (2016), Kate Roberts and Maggie Beattie Roberts help readers write strategies. They encourage teachers to start by thinking of what skill they want to teach their students. "The WHAT is the thing you want students to be able to do at the end of your teaching" (29). Next, you have to think of how students will accomplish the skill you plan to teach. "This HOW is the strategy or the *way* students will perform the skill" (29). Roberts says the HOW can be broken down into a series of three steps. In other words, it is a procedure. Finally, you want to help kids understand WHY they are doing something. In other words, "Why is this strategy important? What is the purpose? Why might we, as readers or writers, want to do this work?" (32). Here's an example of a teaching point that reflects both the skill and its purpose to young writers:

> **THE WHAT + THE HOW + THE WHY** = Writers create paragraphs in stories by making a new paragraph where there is a change in setting—the subway arrives, the sun sets, a week goes by. Paragraphs help readers get a visual heads-up about the changes or shifts coming in the text, so they are ready to experience something new.

**THE WHAT + THE HOW + THE WHY** = Writers study the craft moves of authors to help them revise their essays so their writing emulates writing they admire. Writers study other writers' essays in an effort to try something new and/or lift the level of their own writing so they're continuously becoming stronger writers.

**THE WHAT + THE HOW + THE WHY** = Writers find a writing partner who can help them revise so their writing is the best it can be. Writers ask each other specific questions, rather than taking a pen to each other's papers, to help them fix their own writing. Having a writing partner who asks questions and offers ideas, rather than tells what to do, is important because it allows the writer to think about another perspective while still having control over his or her own writing.

If you use this simple formula (i.e., THE WHAT + THE HOW + THE WHY), you will be able to craft clear teaching points for any strategy you wish to teach your students in a minilesson. When you're crafting teaching points, it's important to word them in a way that helps students add the strategy you've taught to their writing toolbox so they can draw upon it again and again as a writer, rather than feeling as though they're being given an assignment that will help them only with the writing they're working on that given day.

## Final Thoughts

There's no "one way" to teach a whole-class lesson to students. Sometimes a demonstration minilesson will get your point across. Other times you'll want students to discover what a writer did by engaging in an inquiry of a mentor text. On other days you'll want to keep students with you for a longer period of time, so you'll slow down the process with a Your Turn lesson. As you continue to grow your practice as a teacher of writers, you will develop a repertoire of lessons you'll return to again and again. You'll revisit some of your minilessons during the school year in another way. They might become mid-workshop interruptions or be retaught as conferences or small-group lessons or even tweaked for full-class instruction in another unit of study.

## When You're Ready

*Coteaching a Lesson:* If you plan to coteach, you will need to think about what part of a lesson you'll be sharing with your collegue. If you are reading from a mentor text, you might also set the purpose for the day's lesson and model for the students writing in front of them. Your partner may take over to do some brainstorming with the students and then choose an idea from the list to develop a piece of writing as a shared experience. As students move into independent writing, one teacher can circulate as an observer and offer gentle nudges or even do some on-the-spot teaching. The other teacher can remain by the chart and rug where the writing community gathers. Students who need a second go at a shared writing experience, have questions and concerns, or simply need a conversation to get them started can get help from this teacher and leave when they are ready.

*Video Clips of Lessons:* If you are brave, you can videotape each other and "coach" your partner by asking questions and then offer a new strategy, a new resource, or a different format. There is no better way to improve your instruction than by seeing yourself in action. Keep a journal and set some goals after every taping. You and your partner can watch the video together, noting what you saw and heard. On a second viewing, note what you thought or felt.

# Chapter 6

# Independent Writing Time

## The Importance of Giving Students Time to Write

Independent writing time is a sustained thirty to forty-five minutes provided to students every single day to work independently. Ralph Fletcher (2017a) argues it is not the minilesson that is the most important part of writing workshop but rather the block of time we give to our students to write. He suggests the daily schedule we follow each day demonstrates to our students and parents what we value. Regie Routman (2018) explains that volume and effort matter. Students need uninterrupted writing time daily, in all grades. She cautions us that "If we are able to assess all the pages students read and write, they're not reading and writing enough" (174). A much-touted theory in *Outliers: The Story of Success* (Gladwell 2011) proposes that we should practice any skill for ten thousand hours to become proficient.

If we want our writers to be successful, we need to give them the time to practice by actually writing. A regularly scheduled writing workshop—with time for sustained writing—gives students a chance to build their writing muscles. They can start to think about what they would like to write that day. They can talk about it with others before they write. They can plan "next steps" in their head. We cannot skimp on independent time, because kids need uninterrupted periods of time to hone their writing craft to develop the stamina and endurance they need to be strong writers.

**Provide Ample Time for Kids to Produce a Large Volume of Writing**

http://sten.pub/ww18

*Melanie Meehan, Elementary Writing and Social Studies Coordinator*

This sacred writing time is the time you're actively involved in differentiating instruction for all of your students. Although some teachers spend the first few minutes after the minilesson engaging in some writing themselves, most spend the majority of independent writing time teaching their students in highly individualized ways. Here's a breakdown of what's happening from the beginning to the end of independent writing time so you'll have a better sense of what you and your students are doing during this time.

## Give Students a Charge During the Minilesson Link

The last part of every minilesson includes a link, which is a bridge from the minilesson to independent writing time. This is the time when you repeat the teaching point from your minilesson. Often, you'll have a chart with all your recent teaching points that represent strategies you've recently taught to students. You'll remind students that the teaching point you delivered that day is one of their choices for the work they'll do during independent writing time. You may remind students of other strategies you've recently taught, which provide them with possibilities for their focus and direction during that day's work time.

Students should think about the possibilities they have been given. They make a plan—oral or written—for what they will work on that day. Although the minilesson teaching point might be the first thing they choose to focus on that day, it may not be the only thing they work on during independent writing time.

## Period of Silence Is Enforced

The first five to ten minutes of the writing workshop is a time for students to settle into their focus spots so they can start writing. Five to ten (or more) minutes of silence will allow you to jot notes on your clipboard, making plans about who you'll confer with that day. This time allows you to engage in kidwatching. Yetta Goodman (Goodman and Owocki 2002) popularized this term, which is the practice of observing students' activities, noticing how they learn and what they do to explore their ideas. This focused observation provides teachers with authentic measures of children's performance as they engage in writing. During this silent time, you might review your conferring notes to get yourself ready for any conferences or small groups you plan to lead. At the beginning of the school year, you might model good writing behavior by showing students how to settle down and write immediately after the writing lesson. However, doing this on a consistent basis means you will have less time to make observational notes or prepare for the one-on-one conferences and small-group sessions you'll lead that day.

Students engage in silent writing, which allows them to focus on the plan they gave themselves at the end of the minilesson (see Figure 6.1).

**Figure 6.1** These students have elected to sit at desks for the first part of independent writing time.

## Conferring and Small-Group Work Time Begin

You'll be meeting with students one-on-one, in partnerships, or in pairs during this time (see Figure 6.2). (See Chapter 7, "Conferring" and Chapter 8, "Small-Group Instruction.") You'll continue to engage in kidwatching between conferences or the small groups you lead. If students aren't meeting with you or aren't engaged in a peer conference, then they

**Figure 6.2** This teacher is conferring with one of her students in the student's focus spot.

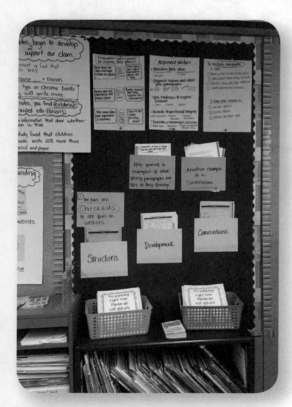

**Figure 6.3** There are a variety of resources students can help themselves to when needed.

are working on the plan they created for the day by writing independently. Students also know that one of the expectations of being a good writer is to constantly be rereading their work and revising. When students need help but you're conferring with a peer, they can access tools around the classroom—anchor charts and interactive pocket charts—to help them get back on track (see Figure 6.3).

## Lead a Mid-Workshop Interruption

Capture your students' attention again, about ten to fifteen minutes into workshop time, by standing in the same place, day after day, to deliver a teaching point that will dramatically raise the level of their work during the workshop time. You'll stop your students by saying, "Writers, may I have your eyes?" and then wait until every student has put down his writing utensil and given you his full attention. Then share a strategy or a reminder with your students that lasts no more than two minutes.

There are three types of mid-workshop points you could make. However, you should choose only one per day to avoid overwhelming students.

- You might deliver a teaching point that builds upon the minilesson teaching point.

- You might choose to highlight something you've noticed one of your students doing that other students may benefit from trying in their own writing. Similarly, you could note what a student has just done that others would benefit from trying.

- You might give the full class a reminder.

The children show you they're listening by having their hands free and maintaining eye contact with you during the brief interruption. After you are finished speaking, students have a go with your suggestion if it pertains to the work they're doing.

## Final Thoughts

Independent writing is a time when you want your students to live a writerly life. This time might help them envision other projects they might want to work on. Real-life writers are always engaged in multiple projects. Therefore, we think it's important to provide your students with opportunities to have an ongoing independent project as their backup work. For some kids, it's using their writer's notebook as a playground. For other kids, it's working in another genre. Regardless of what they're writing, it's important for kids to understand that they can shift gears if they finish their daily plan early. We increase students' agency when they understand they can refocus their attention on an ongoing, independent writing project before the end-of-workshop share session (see Figure 6.4).

## When You're Ready

Our students face many challenges as they take risks and grow as writers. Teachers face many challenges, too, as they try to communicate important tips to help students be successful and confident. One way to free students from routines that are not often helpful is to teach them to reflect on how their draft is going early on. If they have lost interest in their topic or have realized that they are experiencing great difficulty

**Fostering Independence with Classroom Charts**

http://sten.pub/ww19

*Missie Champagne, fourth-grade teacher*

**Mid-Workshop Training**

http://sten.pub/ww20

*Catherine Gehman, fourth-grade teacher*

## When should I abandon a piece of writing?

◆ I don't know enough about the topic to continue, and I don't have the time/ability to research it.

◆ It isn't my story . . . it's someone else's story, and I don't know enough about it.

◆ It's too personal/not appropriate to share with my classmates.

◆ I've lost interest (I can come back to it in the future).

◆ I've changed my mind about the position I initially took on this issue.

**Figure 6.4** With your students, create a list of possible reasons to help them decide when to abandon a piece of writing and start something new.

Scan here for a guide Stacey used with her fourth graders to help them frame their end-of-year letters.

moving forward, it is helpful to know they can abandon a piece of writing and start a new one. This discussion involves important evaluation and reflection. Talk about when to give a piece of writing a second chance, and how to choose topics so carefully and thoughtfully that the chances of abandoning a piece of writing decreases. All writers have false starts. Let's teach children WHEN and WHY it is okay to abandon a piece of writing. Teachers can lead a writerly discussion with students and create an anchor chart with their collective thinking (See Figure 6.4).

At a couple of points during the school year, ask your students to reflect on themselves as writers and learners. Encourage your students to use two days' worth of independent writing time in January to think deeply about the writing work they've done. Tell them their process will help them get to know *themselves* better as writers. You can provide students with a midyear self-evaluation, which you can find an example of in Aimee Buckner's *Notebook Know-How* (2005), to help them guide their reflections.

At the end of the school year, reserve one or two days' worth of independent writing time to have students reflect—in writing—about how the year went by having them write you a letter. Not only will this help them reflect on what they accomplished in your class, but students' feedback will help you grow as a teacher.

# Chapter 7

# Conferring

*Individualize Instruction,
Build Community,
and Set Goals*

All writers need an audience, not only after they have published their writing in some way but at many intervals along their journey from the snow-white page to that joyful feeling they experience when they have created something that is indeed "completed." For the child, there should be nothing more satisfying than the time they spend in a conference. Regie Routman (2005) says there are many purposes for a writing conference, including a time "to celebrate, validate, encourage, nudge, teach, assess, set goals" (206). Purposes for a conference can vary greatly, from helping students focus a topic or opinion piece to coaching students through the process of writing an effective introduction.

Although peer conferences, small-group strategy lessons, and table conferences are doable, helpful, and often a way to save some time, the one-on-one conferences you hold with your students is time well spent. Not only will you get to know your students better as writers (and as people, too), but they will get to know you as a writer. Conferences are a way to build student confidence and resolve some anxieties. Writing is hard work, and some students will need a conference to cheer them on to do the necessary work to grow as a writer. Ralph Fletcher and Joann Porta-lupi (2001) advise us to engage in deep listening and be present, taking in the student's body language and considering the writer's history—all the information you have learned about this student from other conferences and bits of writing. During a conference, you can have a profound influence on how your students approach a draft or revision, discover how motivated they are to write, and understand your students as problem-solvers far better than you ever can from only reading their written work. Talking about planning strategies, topics, and multiple drafts is an essential part of writing, and conferences provide ideal opportunities for that talk (see Figure 7.1).

Of course, conferring is a time when teachers can individualize instruction for every student. It is clear in a one-on-one conference that the student has his teacher's undivided attention and that the teacher will offer praise and instruction.

**Figure 7.1** A fifth-grade teacher confers with a student writer about the concluding paragraph for his literary essay.

The true purpose of any conference is to move the writer, not the piece of writing, forward. It is here we help every student find his writing identity so he believes he can write. We provide support and offer specific feedback. The relationships you forge during one-on-one conference time will help you find pathways to student learning and growth for every student in your classroom (see Figure 7.2).

## Conference Formats

There are several types of conferences we can have when we pull alongside our young writers. Here's a sampling of the kinds of conferences you will try with your students:

## Purposes for a Writing Conference

- To meet the needs of each individual student
- To carve out time to get acquainted with each student, find out interests and assess attitudes
- To mentor and model for students so they can become effective at peer conferring
- To increase motivation to revise
- To provide immediate and ongoing feedback
- To provide a small, non-threatening audience to share writing
- To identify a problem that can be worked on together
- To provide opportunities to ask for immediate clarification
- To teach informally: spelling, sentence structure, punctuation, usage, paragraphing, craft moves, and writing strategies
- To evaluate a student's progress
- To teach students how to self-evaluate
- To set short-term and long-term goals

**Figure 7.2**  One-to-one conferences accomplish many things.

## RESEARCH-DECIDE-TEACH

This kind of conference provides an opportunity for explicit instruction, similar to a minilesson, that is targeted to the needs of one particular student. You can use this kind of conference, popularized by Lucy Calkins (1994), anytime you need or want to do on-the-spot conferring. These conferences last approximately five minutes (see Figure 7.3).

**Research**  You'll spend the first couple of minutes of this kind of conference investigating what the writer is working on by asking her open-ended questions.

# Conferring with Writers Cheat Sheet

### RESEARCH

- What are you working on as a writer?
- How's it going?
- What are you planning to do next and how do you plan for that to go?
- How do you feel about this piece?

- If you were going to fix up this piece of writing to make it much better, what would you do?
- Say more . . .
- Tell me more . . .

### COMPLIMENT

- I want to compliment you. Some people are doing _____, but you're doing _____ . . .

- You're doing really smart work as a writer. I see you . . .
- I noticed the way you're . . .

### TEACH

- You're already doing this work well so I want to give you another tip . . .
- I think you're ready for the next step . . .
- Today I want to teach you . . .
- Watch me as I show you . . .

- One thing I suggest is . . .
- One strategy I use when I write . . .
- Many writers find it helps to . . .
- Let's try this . . .
- Did you notice how . . . ?

### LINK

- What are you going to do next?
- I'd like you to try what we talked about on your own . . .
- I'll be back (after my next conference/in __ minutes) to see how it's going.

- I'm leaving you this (tangible artifact) to remind you of the strategy we worked on today.
- Keep going!

**Figure 7.3** Here are some phrases to help you work through your Research-Decide-Teach conferences with writers.

**Decide** Once you've pursued a couple lines of questioning with the writer you're meeting with, it's time to decide what to teach her. You'll want to think of *one* thing to compliment and *one* strategy for instruction. Lucy Calkins urges teachers to think, "What is the most important way I can help this child to become a dramatically better writer?" (2013, 75). It's okay to take a moment to think so you can make the best teaching decision. Before you launch into your teaching, take the time to give the child a compliment. The compliment should be specific and focus on a skill you've observed. Be genuine and respond with emotion, saying what you saw or noticed rather than what you liked or loved about what the child did. (The latter places a value judgment on the child and makes her more dependent upon your praise in the future.) Often your compliment will teach into the upper edge of what a child is doing as a writer. It's important to understand an emerging strength when a writer demonstrates partial understanding of a writing skill (Anderson 2018a). By noting a partial understanding, you recognize a strategy a child is trying with some strength. By complimenting it, you increase the likelihood of moving the child further forward as a writer. A solid compliment should be about a paragraph of speech (e.g., five sentences long), recognizing the child for what she accomplished so she can replicate it again and again.

You might link your compliment to your teaching point by saying, "You're already doing this work well, so I want to give you another tip" or "I think you're ready for the next step." Language like this recognizes what a young writer is already trying so they are encouraged and ready to try something a little bigger as a writer (Clements 2017).

**Teach** Next, you'll teach the writer in front of you *how* to do something better as a writer. Most of the time you'll do this by demonstrating the step-by-step process or by giving an explanation with an example. When you demonstrate, you'll use a piece of writing (e.g., your writing, a student's writing, or a published text) to help the student envision what you're asking them to try on their own.

Stay—for a minute or two—while the child tries the strategy you taught her. Before you step away from the writer so she can work independently, you'll want to link back to your teaching point, stressing the transference of your teaching point to the child's independent writing process or her toolbox of strategies. To do this, you might leave behind a tangible artifact—such as a sticky note or a premade label—that reflects the teaching point of your conference. You might also establish a time (e.g., later in the workshop, the next day) to follow up with the writer. Touching base—even if it's quick—helps students to be accountable for the things you teach them in a writing conference.

## STRATEGIC

This kind of conference provides explicit instruction on one strategy based on a student's writing goals (Anderson 2008). You should use this kind of conference once you've established writing goals for all of your students. Like a Research-Decide-Teach conference, this conference lasts approximately five minutes.

Strategic conferring is a lot like the way a primary care physician practices medicine. Your primary care doctor knows who you are and the health issues you have and comes into your appointment informed about what's been happening since your last checkup. The doctor may still ask you questions at the beginning of the visit, but they're focused questions based on the doctor's knowledge of you as a patient. His or her knowledge of your medical history helps guide the questioning and leads to better outcomes for your health.

Like doctors, we have writing goals for students that help us anticipate where we might go when we confer with them. Our goals for students help us find a focus during the research part of the conference. Over time, we look to see how students are doing with those goals and adjust our teaching to help students meet them (Anderson 2011).

Essentially, as teachers, we should review our conferring notes before we sit down with a student. Using the goals that have already been set for our student writers (preferably alongside them), we can guide them in the proper direction. We continue to check in with our students about their writing goals periodically so we can move them forward as writers. Over time, we work on a few things to help our young writers get stronger (Shubitz 2011).

## COACHING

This conference supports a writer who is struggling with a concept and needs help through a particular part of the writing process. You'll use this kind of conference when you need to set the child up for success at the end of the conference. Keep a close eye on the time during a coaching conference so you don't spend more than seven minutes with the student. Longer than seven minutes usually means the child probably won't add the strategy you're teaching to his writing toolbox after you depart.

You can think of coaching conferences like a coach calling to the players while a game is in progress. You're instructing the student with a writing strategy, by whispering lean and succinct prompts, while engaging the child as he tries the strategy. Like the football coach who helps players from the sidelines, whisper in to the writer rather than taking control of the writing. Remember, the person who is holding the pen is doing the thinking! Students with pens in hand are doing the thinking work they need to do so they can succeed with a minimal amount of teacher support.

## MENTOR TEXT

This conference provides you with an opportunity to study a text and teach a student a strategy that will lift the level of his work. You will engage in a mentor text conference when you want to set the agenda by studying a text alongside a writer. You can do this in two ways. First, you can use inquiry where you invite a student to study a text with you, which enables the student to discover the craft, name what he noticed, and transfer it to his own writing. Second, you show the student an example of a craft move an author made and provide an explanation of how to make that move (Shubitz 2016). Like many of the other conferences you lead, these conferences last approximately five minutes.

**Poetry Coaching Conference**

http://sten.pub/ww21

*Frank Murphy, sixth-grade teacher*

## COMPLIMENT-ONLY

One of the best ways to raise the energy level or confidence of a writer is to hold a compliment-only conference. You can use the following template, which was originated by Shana Frazin of the Teachers College Reading and Writing Project, for structuring this kind of conference:

- "I notice . . ."
- "This matters because . . ."
- "So anytime you are writing . . ."

Lanny Ball (2017) gives the following advice:

> *When using this template, begin by providing a precise description of something the writer has done (hopefully repeatedly). Preferably this statement emphasizes a move we see writers in the world using to help their pieces be more effective. ("I notice you . . .") Follow this with an explanation as to why writers employ such a technique ("This matters because . . ."). Finally, you can end your compliment-only conference by looking into the writer's eyes and letting him know that you hope he will continue to rely on this move anytime he is doing this type of writing ("So anytime you are writing . . .").*

A word of caution: We still need to hold conferences where we're teaching writers a new strategy. However, you can use this kind of conference when you wish to reinforce the exemplary work a child is already doing by noticing and naming it for him.

## STICKY NOTE

Sometimes you're short on time but need to reach all of your students in a given day. Sticky-note conferences are non-verbal conferences where you write a note to a student about what she is doing well or what she should work on immediately. This allows you to cruise around the classroom to interact with each student by providing them with meaningful and immediate feedback. Spending about one minute per student, you will be able to reach all of your students during independent writing time on a given day.

Although you can use sticky-note conferences anytime, they are often best used on a day when all of your students are doing the same kind of work (e.g., on a collecting day at the start of a new unit of study). It's likely all of your students will be in the same kind of place and will need lots of uninterrupted time to just write, which makes these non-verbal conferences effective and efficient.

## TABLE

Like sticky-note conferences, table conferences are held when most or all of your students are at the same place in a unit of study, which is typically when you're beginning a new unit. Therefore, moving from table to table in your classroom is an excellent way to reach a lot of students on the same day.

Anna Gratz Cockerille (2014) says, "To conduct a table conference, start by taking a quick peek at the students sitting at one table or in one cluster of desks. Notice if there are one or two teaching points that could benefit most of the writers in the group. Then, choose one student who exemplifies the kind of thing others in the group need help with. Ask the student if he minds if others listen while you confer with him and invite the rest of the table to eavesdrop on your discussion." We must shift back and forth between conferring with one child and debriefing the work she is doing by saying things such as "Do you see how Anthony just did such-and-so? Try doing the same thing right now" (Calkins 2013, 55). Once the students sitting at the same table have tried what their peer has done well, the teacher can ask them to try the same teaching point she delivered to the child she focused on during the table conference.

Not every student at the table may benefit from your teaching point, but that's okay. It's likely you're reinforcing something you've already taught or something the other writers are doing well. It's important to remember that reinforcement and reteaching will not harm your writers.

## Peer Conferences

To help your workshop run more efficiently, it is a good idea to train your students to confer with their peers. Perhaps the best way to start is to have two students work together daily throughout a unit of study (or even for a semester or an entire school year) to help each other as writers (see Figure 7.4). Peer conferences can take place once you've had the opportunity to teach social skills so students can collaborate effectively. Social skills can include taking turns, using each other's names, keeping eyes focused on the speaker, disagreeing in an agreeable way, encouraging others with verbal and nonverbal communications, and self-assessing the work that is accomplished during peer conferences. See the QR code on the next page for an example of peer conference.

**Figure 7.4** These students have worked as writing partners during a fourth-grade unit of study on argument essays.

According to Kathleen Tolan (2015), there are two kinds of peer conferring:

- *One student teaches, the other student learns.* Sometimes Partner A is stronger than Partner B is at something (e.g., focusing their writing). The student with the stronger skill might teach their partner how to get better at something. Another time Partner B might be stronger than Partner A at something (e.g., elaborating with a variety of details). That's when Partner B gets to step into the teacher role to teach Partner A how to do something better. One partner is always helping their partner become more proficient at something.

- *Partners learn alongside each other to get better at a skill.* Sometimes both members of a partnership aren't proficient with an aspect of writing (e.g., writing with voice). Together they decide to work together to get better at doing the thing they're both struggling with (in this case, making their writing sound like themselves).

This is similar to two colleagues learning together to get better at something (e.g., how to teach the *Units of Study* better). If your classroom community is grounded in growth mindset, then this kind of peer conferring is powerful, because students are engaged in their learning and are problem-solving together to become stronger writers.

Here are some tips for making peer conferences work in your classroom:

1. *Show students videos of successful peer conferences.* Lead a discussion about what worked, what they noticed these writers doing, and how they could transfer what they observed the partners in the video doing to the work they do with their writing partner. Watch the video by scanning the QR code for an example of a peer conference.

2. *Employ the P, Q, P Technique.* Jim Vopat suggested the Praise, Question, Polish Technique (2007). It's a good way to get kids who are new to peer conferring started with providing each other with compliments and critical feedback.

3. *Fishbowl great conferences.* You can do one of two things when you notice a partnership engaged in a powerful peer conference. You can stop your entire class and invite them to listen and watch what their peers are doing. If you'd prefer not to stop everyone, record the conference on your smartphone and show it to your entire class during share time.

4. *Provide time for partners to meet.* Working with a writing partner a couple times a week helps build rapport among writers (Shubitz 2015). However, Mark Overmeyer (2017) suggests that peer conferences should be in the hands of the writer. That is, the writer decides *when* to confer with a peer and *why* to confer with a peer. Overmeyer suggests that when we allow students to schedule their own peer conferences, we provide students with another opportunity for choice. All students need support at different parts of the writing process. If students decide when they need a peer conference, peer conferences become more authentic learning opportunities.

This video is called *Peer Conferring: Students Teach Each Other to Revise in Order to Orient their Readers (3–5)* and comes from the Teachers College Reading and Writing Project's Vimeo Page.

5. *Focus on content, not conventions.* Peer conferences should be based on idea generation, content, craft, and process rather than on editing skills (Overmeyer 2015). Elementary students listen to each other and often introduce errors as they're editing each other's work. Since editing should be done by the writer, save editing conventions for a time when kids have your support rather than each other's (see Figure 7.5).

## SELF-CONFERENCES

Self-conferences are opportunities for writers to engage in the close reading of their texts and to be the first reader of their work. The first self-conference happens after a student has completed a draft, and sometimes before the first draft is finished. Reading his piece both silently and aloud, the student can discover where he forgot to write a word or a sentence that does not read smoothly. Sometimes, he can discover sentences that weaken his focus and do not belong at all. After a conference with the teacher or a peer, a student holds another self-conference to determine what revision or editing he will need to do. A student can use a rubric or checklist to guide the self-conference, but it isn't always necessary. Training students to "read like writers" is important so they can see their own work as critics.

## Conference Roles

Students and teachers play different roles in conferences. Figure 7.6 on page 108 shows a chart of expectations to help you teach your students how a conference goes.

## Classroom Management

"There are too many children in this classroom! And there is so much content to cover! How am I ever going to fit in time to confer with each student?"

Classrooms that are student-centered and project-based grow students who are independent learners. Once you think your students know what they can do during writing workshop, you can begin to confer daily.

Title of Writing: _____

Genre: _____

Author's Name: _____ Peer's Name: _____

## *P* is for *praise*.

Be specific. Tell the writer one thing s/he did well:

_____

_____

_____

_____

## *Q* is for *question*.

Do you have any questions after reading this piece? If so, write down the most important question for the writer here:

_____

_____

_____

_____

## *P* is for *polish*.

Tell the writer ONE thing s/he can do to make his/her writing better. (Think: title, intro paragraph, show not tell, concluding paragraph, adding more dialogue, editing, etc.) _____

_____

_____

**Figure 7.5** You may use a tool like this to help students get used to peer conferring. Like any scaffold, this is a temporary tool, and helps students confer with a peer. Once students become proficient with peer conferring, you can fade out the use of a tool like this to help students get started with the P, Q, P Technique.

| Teacher's Role | Student's Role |
| --- | --- |
| • Set an agenda for the conference (often collaboratively with the writer).<br><br>• Ask open-ended questions to figure out what the child is working on as a writer (not what he is writing).<br><br>• Actively listen to the child so he can help you figure out what to teach him.<br><br>• Compliment the writer on something he is doing well.<br><br>• Teach the writer one strategy that will move him forward as a writer.<br><br>• Provide time for the child to ask questions while they're having a go with the strategy you taught.<br><br>• Jot notes about the conference using your record-keeping tool of choice so you can monitor progress and plan for future instruction.<br><br>• Leave behind a tangible artifact—using pictures and/or words—that reflects what you taught the student. | • Explain what he is doing as a writer, rather than telling you what he is writing.<br><br>• Actively listen to what the teacher is saying and ask questions if confused.<br><br>• Try out the strategy that is presented.<br><br>• (Upper elementary students) Jot notes about what they learned in their writer's notebook.<br><br>• Apply the strategy to this piece of writing and future pieces of writing when applicable. |

**Figure 7.6** Teacher and student roles in a writing conference

## WHERE TO CONFER

Around the Classroom: You might choose to move around the classroom to confer with students at their seats or in their focus spots. Moving around the room means you'll need a conferring toolkit (see end of chapter) to help you keep your materials organized as you move from student to student. Having the teacher move around the classroom during independent writing time minimizes the number of children walking around. In addition, meeting students wherever they're sitting is an excellent management technique: students never know where you'll be, so it encourages them to stay on-task. Here, it is good to have eye contact with the students, so you will need to sit beside the child or carry a travel seat—something light that can help you be comfortable—as you're moving around the classroom to confer.

In One Space: First, you will need to find a place away from your desk—if you have one—where you can confer sitting beside the student, preferably in a chair that does not make you tower above your students. Look for a space in your classroom that is quiet and pleasant. Sometimes, you have to create one by using bookshelves and other furniture to create a cozy nook.

Finding a Spot with a Partner: In an effort to help kids receive a variety of feedback, you can encourage students to occasionally move around the classroom to confer with different peers. A conference clock can be used to pair students, build community, and create opportunities for peer conferences. Closely monitored by the teacher, students have several minutes to "make an appointment" with two or three classmates. The "clock" is divided into four quadrants. When a student signs up for a conference in a time slot, his chosen partner also fills in the time slot on his conference clock. Then the student tries to make one or two more "appointments," each with a different peer. The teacher has a system to let students know they have a minute left to make their final appointments and how many appointments they will make altogether. Then, students find a spot in the classroom to sit and confer with their first appointment, often using a praise-ponder-polish format. The polish notes are written on sticky notes and offered to the partner. After all appointments have been honored,

**Teacher and Student Roles in a Conference**

http://sten.pub/ww22

*Melanie Meehan, Elementary Writing and Social Studies Coordinator*

students return to their seat to write their reflections in the last quadrant of the clock. These reflections can be shared in whole group to close the workshop. This reflection may simply talk about a polish that was used to revise a piece, a ponder that helped the writer make a change or add a detail, or a praise that was specific and helped the writer recognize a strength. Conference clocks work best with students in third through sixth grades. They are important because they help students understand all the writers in their community can offer valuable feedback, not just their best friends or the students who sit next to them. Conference clocks promote the idea that the entire writing community can function as a giant think tank (see Chapter 9, "Share Sessions").

To help manage conference clocks, regularly check them to see whether the student writers are choosing the same or different conference buddies. It is important to encourage them to seek feedback from myriad community members. This practice helps students see all their classmates as writers and strengthens the social dimension of the classroom (see Figure 7.7).

## Time for a Conference

To keep to your time limit, we suggest setting a stopwatch when each conference begins. Strive to keep conferences three to seven minutes in length. Occasionally, you will bend this rule for a student who is inspired or needs a little more prodding to be inspired. If you have twenty-five students in your classroom, you will need to hold about five conferences daily to see everyone in the span of one week.

Some teachers find it helpful to use a Class-at-a-Glance grid to keep track of the students they've met with in a given week. Blank boxes serve as a reminder to check in with students who haven't had a writing conference that week. Other teachers might use a visual conference tracker—which all students can see—to help them keep track of kids they've met with for a conference in a given week (Shubitz 2007). A conference tracker can be created out of foam core and clothespins. The foam core can be divided in half: waiting for a conference or had a conference. As you meet

Determining Student Readiness for a Conference

http://sten.pub/ww23

*Lesley Turner, fifth-grade teacher*

with each child, you can move their clothes-pin from the "waiting for a conference" side to the "had a conference" side so you can distribute your time equitably among your students each week. At the end of each week, you can shift all the clothespins back to the "waiting for a conference" side so you can start fresh the following week.

## Volume Level

Students must know each writer's confer-ence time needs to be respected; therefore, no interruptions are allowed unless it is

**Figure 7.7** Sitting beside a student makes it easier to not only view his writing but have a conversation at eye level.

an emergency. Students also need to use their whisper voices if they are holding a peer conference somewhere else in the room or reading their piece aloud as a self-check. For the most part, pencils should be sharpened at the start of the morning and right after lunch, and trips to the bathroom should be limited. Sometimes, a voice-level chart can be posted in a promi-nent place for all to see. This chart can be created during a writerly discus-sion during the fall. If writing workshop is too noisy, it is hard for anyone to concentrate during conference time. Volume levels for a chart can include no-talking time (zero), a six-inch voice for conferences (Level One), a regu-lar speaking voice for discussions/shares (Level Two), a presentation voice (Level Three), and an outside-recess voice (Level Four).

## Developing Writing Stamina

Finally, it is important to develop writing stamina. Students must be able to commit to longer and longer periods of sustained silent writing. To that end, one management technique is to place a banner on the board (you can use magnets to hold it up) or another location visible to all that says something such as "Shhhh! Everybody's writing!" While the banner is in view, students are silent, reviewing their writer's notebook, planning, sketching, drafting.

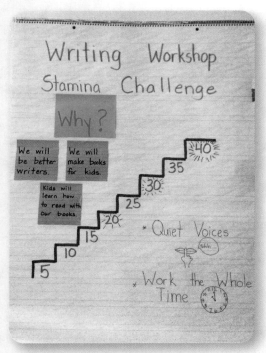

**Figure 7.8** Young writers can build stamina over time.

No pencils are being sharpened. No one is up and moving about. No one is conferring. This quiet time may be about five to ten minutes long; it's your call. It is crucial for writers who need the think time and the silence to start writing before the classroom dissolves into various activities.

Students need to develop writing fluency to have writing stamina. A simple technique is to place an X somewhere on a writer's page and ask the student to try to "write to the X" during the day's workshop. When the student meets that goal, move the X farther down the page. Another idea for increasing students' stamina is to track and record how much time they were able to remain quiet during independent writing time. If you want your students to have the patience to write for longer stretches of time, it's important to build their stamina in five-minute increments (Shubitz 2016). If the goal is to get kids to write independently for forty-five minutes, they have to work up to it. A chart like the one Betsy Hubbard uses is as effective with helping fourth graders build stamina as it is with kindergartners. All kids can write for longer stretches of time if they work up to it (see Figure 7.8).

## Conference Requests from Students

Sometimes students will request a conference with you, so you'll want to create a sign-up system on something like a laminated chart. As a student finishes his conference with you, he will go to the chart and cross out his name. It is his job to tap the shoulder of the next person on the list. Students should never be standing in a long line at the conference table waiting for their conference time to come up; their eyes should be on their writing! Another option is to have a container filled with conference request cards (see Chapter 4, "Classroom Management") that are folded to create a tent that can be displayed on a student's desk. Yet another option is to simply create and post a schedule with assigned times. Students can say "pass" if they are not ready, and you can place an asterisk by their name to move them to the front of the next day's schedule.

If you want to keep your scheduled conferences short, make sure your students are reading their pieces aloud and silently before they come to you. This is important! Writers should always be the first readers of their work. They should be prepared for a conference and ready to ask for specific help. You should not be doing all the talking. If you are the first reader during the conference and read aloud to the student writer, the writer can be the first speaker. He will often recognize what needs immediate improvement just from listening to his own words. *Your* vocalization of the piece is at least the second time the writer should have heard his work, because he is the first reader. Sometimes, writers fill in missing words naturally as they read as well as details they know in their head that may not be on the paper. That is why your vocalization of the text is so important: you won't be doing that!

## Mentor Texts

Make sure your mentor texts are close by so you can refer to them during your conferences. A paperback copy can be placed in the classroom library for students to access independently. Sometimes you will want to refer a student to a particular craft move. During conference time, a mentor text is not shared in its entirety—just the part the student needs, since a mentor text is something the student has usually heard at least once before. Sometimes, a genre, subgenre (i.e., fables), or form (i.e., feature article) has been studied in class, so a mentor text that could be part of that study may be new to the student, but the genre or form is not. Mentor texts are often picture books, but they can be poems, song lyrics, articles, essays, travel brochures, and even cookbooks! A file of mentor texts by genre and form can serve teacher and student well. Including student writing as mentor texts is often helpful.

**Goal-Setting Conference**

http://sten.pub/ww24

*Kolleen Bell, Kindergarten Teacher*

## PUBLISHED MENTOR TEXTS

The number of mentor texts you use during each school year may vary, but a collection of fifteen to twenty-five will serve you well. Make sure the collection includes a variety of authors, genres, and formats. Choose the ones you love and the ones that best fit the needs of your current class. They serve to provide your students with gentle nudges to take risks and try new things. Picture books are easy for you to use in a conference with your students, and they are also easy for students to refer to independently when they are drafting and revising.

## STUDENT-WRITTEN MENTOR TEXTS

For conferring purposes, have a folder of each writing type (informational, narrative, opinion/argument) containing several student mentor texts (from this year or previous years) with you as you move around your classroom to confer. Be ready to share one or two when students need another exemplar or just need to see that students at their grade level can use a certain strategy or craft move. A student-written mentor text is often more believable for reluctant and struggling writers. Students will gain confidence in their writing when they hear student examples of great work, so they will come to understand it's not only published authors who write well—they can look to their peers for mentor texts, too.

## TEACHER-WRITTEN MENTOR TEXTS

It is important to be a teacher of writers who writes! When we share our stories, poems, and notebook entries with our students, we become more real to them. We immerse ourselves in the process, and we discover that creating our own mentor texts for our students will provide clear guidelines of our expectations. When we write in front of our students and get stuck, they will help us out. It's wonderful for them to see us struggle, to see that we don't always get it right the first time and that we can benefit from suggestions from our fellow writers—our students—too. Our teacher-written mentor texts make us believable and put us inside the writing community. Dorfman and Cappelli (2017) tell us, "We need to write so that we can call ourselves 'author'" (13).

# Conference Record-Keeping

Record-keeping is important because it helps you distribute your time equitably among students. Keeping good records allows you to see the tracks of your teaching and monitor student growth. In addition, it helps you determine next steps with each student, small groups, or the whole class, which is crucial if you're going to engage in strategic conferring with your students.

You can jot your notes down at two different times while you're conferring. One option is to write your notes while the student is actively engaged with the strategy you've taught. Another option is to record your notes between conferences with different students. Some teachers take notes with a pen and paper, whereas others prefer to house their conferring records digitally using Evernote or Google Drive. There's no one right way to keep conferring notes. It is important for you to determine the best method system to do the following:

- Hold yourself accountable to teaching in ways that have traction.
- Collect and consolidate large-scale data, so you can see patterns and trends across a class (or all your classes) and can teach whole-class and small-group instruction in response.
- Track an individual writer's progress, seeing evidence of growth (or lack thereof), so your upcoming work with that writer can be informed by what you see and so that writer knows you are attending to his progress.
- Help writers track their own progress toward goals by teaching them to record what they are learning, what they are working toward, and achievements they've made (Calkins, Hohne, and Robb 2015, 61).

Because learning environments differ somewhat based on factors such as student ages, levels of proficiency, and access to technology, we have included a variety of record-keeping forms in Appendix D.

## PAPER NOTES

There are endless ways you can use paper to keep records of your conferences. Some teachers jot notes on a weekly Class-at-a-Glance grid, which they keep on a clipboard or on the front page of their conferring binder. Each child has a box on the grid where the teacher records the child's name, the date, a compliment, and a teaching point. Blank boxes serve as a reminder for teachers to check in with students who haven't had a writing conference that week. When Stacey was a classroom teacher, she used a three-ring binder, which had tabs for each student. In each student's section, goals appeared on the top of the page and she jotted notes in a four-column chart, which included the date, her compliment, her teaching point, and next steps for each student. Her notes allowed her to track each writer's progress so she could see evidence of growth over time. Having "next steps" allowed Stacey to plan for future conferences or to group students together for strategy lessons.

Some teachers use notebooks, which they divide into sections for each student. From there, they take freehand notes every time they meet with a student. Kolleen Bell has a folder in which she jots her conferring notes on sticky notes (see Figure 7.9). At the end of each week, she removes the sticky notes and transfers them into a notebook, which has pages for each student. Using that information, she looks for commonalities to drive her small-group instruction and help her plan for full-class instruction. Regardless of how you keep notes—on sheets of paper, in a notebook, on sticky notes—it's important to find a system with which you're comfortable. Be prepared to try many different systems before settling on one that works for you.

## HIGH-TECH NOTES

Your notebook, tablet, or laptop can also be handy while you confer to save student writing samples, to record conferences, to create digital portfolios, and to communicate with families about their child's progress as a writer.

**Figure 7.9** Record-keeping with sticky notes

## STUDENT WRITING

Rather than photocopying student writing to save for future reference, apps such as Scannable make it easy to digitally scan and save high-quality images of student writing. Stacey has found Evernote to be particularly helpful for filing student writing samples. You can snap a photo of any piece of student writing and save it in a note within Evernote. This is useful because you can see what a child was working on on any given day. In addition, you can photograph the work of several children you wish to highlight in some way and who represent the writers in your class—during different parts of the writing process—so you can have student-written mentor texts to use with future students. Evernote's notebook and tagging features make it easy to save student writing samples.

## VOICE RECORDINGS

Use your device to record a conference. Voice recordings are fantastic because they allow you to capture the time you spent with a student and help you analyze the teaching you did. For instance, you can listen to a conference to determine whether you taught the important thing the writer needed. If you didn't, then you can think of how to improve your decision about what to teach the next time. (Perhaps you need to research longer for the right teaching point to become apparent.) In addition, you might record a student reading part of her writing that she fixed as a result of your teaching. This can be preserved as a note in your digital conferring notebook and then shared with the class or the child's family as a way to showcase her hard work. There are many voice recorder apps available. Evernote users can record multiple audio clips within a note on the app, which you can access on all your devices.

## DIGITAL PORTFOLIOS

Digital portfolios are defined as online collections of learning artifacts created to showcase a student's accomplishments and growth over time. With the availability and ease of use of digital tools today, there are many benefits to using this authentic process of assessment. For example, a student can talk about how this piece demonstrated that he took some risks and tried something new. Another piece can demonstrate the writer's strengths or how he problem solved. Artifacts can be collected with Google Drive Digital Portfolios, and when student work is housed in an online space for others to see, parents, peers, and even the larger community can provide authentic audiences and feedback. Digital portfolios can also serve as a tool for formative assessment and can be treated as a student-driven assessment experience. In other words, students can take ownership for the selection of artifacts to be included in their portfolio and tag them with reflections that discuss why they chose each one.

## HOME-SCHOOL CONNECTIONS

Technology tools offer great potential for connecting home and school. Edmodo and Seesaw can provide a virtual window into your classroom. A free service for teachers and students, they are an easy way to get students connected so they can safely collaborate, get and stay organized, and access assignments, grades, and school messages. With an access code, parents can join the space to view and comment on their child's writing and have access to important links and resources.

Also, for teachers using Evernote, it's easy to share your individual conferring notes with parents when a conference has gone well and you wish to celebrate a student's success beyond the classroom community.

## CHECKLISTS

Teachers need a useful tool during conferences to track student progress. Checklists can be useful in several ways. You can record notes on them and sometimes simply check off parts of the list. Later, you can look through the notes and the checked-off information to create a new list of teaching points for minilessons. Another way to use this information is to look for similar needs to help you create small-group conferences or small, flexible groups for instruction. Checklists can also be used to highlight both process and product. Some teachers use two different colors to denote strengths and weaknesses. Another way to use a checklist is to look only at process or only at product.

## ON-DEMAND ASSESSMENTS

After you give students an on-demand assessment (e.g., before a unit of study begins to determine what the children already know and can do, or at the end of a unit to determine what skills students have mastered and what needs further instruction), it's important to mine the students' writing for patterns. Stacey recorded each child's strengths and areas of need on a

**Professional Learning Communities Work Together to Assess Student Writing**

http://sten.pub/ww25

*Betsy Gunsalus, Director of Elementary Curriculum and Student Assessment*

For more information about creating toolkits, check out "A Peek Inside Conferring Toolkits," a series of blog entries on the *Two Writing Teachers* website.

sticky note, which she attached to the front page of each child's on-demand assessment. These notes helped her determine whether students had met their writing goals and what else they needed to work on. Regardless of whether you assess using the 6+1 Traits Rubric from Education Northwest, the Learning Progressions from the Teachers College Reading and Writing Project, or something else your school provides, it's important to make sure the information you glean from each student's on-demand writing drives your one-to-one conferring with them in the weeks to come. Once you're finished, you might store students' on-demand writing in a three-ring binder or scan their pieces and save them in digital folders.

## Toolkits

Conferring toolkits are organizational systems that help keep your writing workshop materials in one place (see Figure 7.10). Having a well-stocked toolkit allows you to confer with ease so you aren't running across your classroom looking for sticky notes or a mentor text while you're conferring with your students wherever they're sitting. Some teachers use a zippered three-ring portfolio (basically a twenty-first-century version of a Trapper Keeper) to help them keep their conferring records, cheat sheets, checklists, mini-charts, mentor texts, and supplies in one place. Teachers who use tablets to store their conference records and mentor texts may wish to place those items in a tote bag and carry it from student to student as they confer so that their office supplies (e.g., sticky notes, spider legs, pens, and highlighters) are all in one place.

## Final Thoughts

Writing conferences are conversations where we exude warmth while teaching students something new to add to their writing repertoire. Carl Anderson (2018b) talks about being an optimistic writing teacher, one who is able to see students' partial understandings, which is critical to teaching children well. When we notice and note a student's emerging strengths in a writing conference, we transform a partial understanding into an

## Conferring Toolkit Contents

- Lists of students' writing goals
- Conferring notes
- Conferring menus
- Checklist and/or rubric
- Mentor texts you've studied with your students
- Your own writing (multiple copies so you can leave them with students)
- Former students' published writing (multiple copies so you can leave them with students)
- Student work samples for all stages of the writing process
- Small copies of shared writing or class stories
- Mini-charts
- Small, typed-up versions of anchor charts you've displayed during minilessons
- Portable word wall
- Transition word/phrases list
- Reminder cards (e.g., tangible artifacts to leave behind at the end of a conference)

### OFFICE SUPPLIES

- Glue stick, mini stapler, and/or Scotch tape
- Highlighters
- Loose-leaf paper and/or legal pad
- Magic Markers
- Paperclips
- Pens/pencils
- Scrap paper
- Spider legs or index cards (for revision)
- Sticky notes
- Your writer's notebook
- Tab the pages where you collected and nurtured your idea

Idea adapted from Jennifer Serravallo (2006).

**Figure 7.10** Conferring toolkit contents

opportunity to teach a student how to do something new as a writer, which will help the child develop a more complete understanding. If we aim to make our conferences supportive and joyful, we build students up as both people and writers.

## When You're Ready

It's useful to have a bank of student-written mentor texts for all points of the writing process for every unit of study you teach. Select three to five students—or children you wish to highlight because they are a good representation of the kinds of writers in your classroom—whose work you'll track during a unit of study (Ayres and Shubitz 2010). Photocopy or scan (scanning is better, because you'll have digital records of their work) their writing at every stage of the writing process: from collecting entries in their notebook to first draft to published piece. Keeping these samples will provide you with a bank of mentor texts you can pull out anytime in the future to teach a strategy to future students.

For more ideas about how to use student writing as mentor texts, read *Learning from Classmates: Using Students' Writing as Mentor Texts* by Lisa Eickholdt (2015) and *We Can Do This! Student Mentor Texts That Teach and Inspire* by Janiel Wagstaff (2017).

# Chapter 8

# Small-Group Instruction

## *High Value, High Reward*

Although whole-group instruction is an essential part of instruction, it has its limitations. It often results in teaching "to the middle" and doesn't provide what all students—for instance, striving writers and high achievers—need to grow as writers. Small-group work helps solve this issue and is part of the essential work we do in writing workshop. Small-group instruction makes it possible for every student to have a voice in the learning and assessment process, especially those students who are shy or even a little afraid to share their thoughts with the whole group. Small-group instruction is often based on the need to accomplish short-term goals.

Creating small groups for students to interact with one or more peers has many benefits besides building and sustaining a learning community. Small groups increase engagement, helping all learners play an active role. But grouping can be challenging. Many teachers will resort to whole-group instruction for everything or form groups where students remain static. They stay in the same group for weeks, months, or even the entire year. Opportunities to learn from and develop relationships with all their classmates does not often happen in this kind of setting. On the other hand, flexible grouping organizes students intentionally and fluidly for different learning experiences over a relatively short period of time. Students are grouped with task and purpose in mind, often by using classroom assessment results, including daily formative assessment practices, students' interests, and students' attitudes as criteria. "Teachers who adjust to meet the needs of all students manipulate grouping options to maximize learning" (Radencich, McKay, and Parratore, 1995, 25).

Small-group instruction can help students explore and share ideas they may not be able to in the classroom. Teachers can function in many ways during small-group instruction. Sometimes they present a strategy in a way that's different from how it was presented to the whole group. This extra help is for students who might understand the strategy on some level but

**Figure 8.1** A third-grade teacher works with a small group to reinforce the teaching point presented in the minilesson.

have not used it in their writing pieces. The small-group instruction provides the extra practice that will give them the confidence to try it on their own (see Figure 8.1).

## How Small-Group Instruction Differs from Conferring

The purpose of small-group instruction is to reteach a concept or to teach a new strategy based on the information a teacher has gathered through conferences and assessments of written work. Small-group instruction can be used to match writers to work as a team toward a short-term goal while it's often used for intervention purposes, small-group instruction can be used just as often for enrichment and challenge. Whatever the purpose, small-group instruction builds peer relationships and mentorships that extend beyond the small-group structure.

Both small-group instruction and conferring are based on the principles of differentiation. As Tomlinson (2001) says, differentiation is student centered, energetic, and deeply rooted in assessment. Both individual conferences and small-group instruction stand on these principles. In a conference, we meet our students where they currently are and respond to their questions and needs. They tend to be more spontaneous in nature. In small-group instruction, the teacher has already determined the focus and purpose of the small group. Like a one-to-one conference, small-group sessions provide opportunities for immediate practice of the strategy being taught with the security of a small group of peers and a teacher to provide support when necessary. One-on-one conferring is at the heart of the writing workshop, but many of our classes have twenty to thirty (or more!) students. We cannot rely on conferring alone to teach strategies explicitly, since many students need greater frequency, support, and practice.

Small, flexible groups help teachers differentiate instruction. When teachers examine their conference notes, their anecdotal observations of daily progress, and information students provide for anchor charts during instruction or after whole-group discussions, they can decide which students might benefit from a small-group gathering.

Small-group instruction makes it possible to differentiate while still providing highly individualized instruction in ways that will meet all students' needs. It's always a good idea to start out by telling your small group something you've noticed that they are doing well. Then move to what you have noticed in conferences, class discussions, or student work that needs to be addressed. Introduce the strategy or craft move you will explore together. Do some teaching and move into independent practice with coaching (see Figure 8.2).

**Figure 8.2** A fourth-grade teacher meets with a small group of students about the plan boxes they created for independent writing time.

Finally, as your students leave you, encourage them to continue the work you taught them in their writer's notebook or current draft. Transfer is the universal principle of teaching!

In small-group instruction, teachers play an active role. They are the experts and can teach or nudge the students to try a new strategy or craft move within the safe environment of a small-group setting with the expectation that students will try to incorporate it in some way in their current drafts. Through demonstration, questions and interactive discussions, small groups move students toward greater independence.

## Types of Small-Group Instruction

### STRATEGY GROUPS

Small-group strategy lessons aren't just for the writers who are endeavoring the most. All kids need to work in small groups anytime they are struggling to carry out a particular skill independently. As teachers, we support students by pulling them for strategy lessons in groups of three to five and teaching them a strategy for mastering the skill.

When forming small groups, it is important to think about whether you can move your students forward as writers in one session or will need to meet with them for a series of small-group lessons.

Your small groups can consist of inexperienced, midrange, and sophisticated writers who are demonstrating the same need on a given day. It's important to be flexible with your groupings, because they are not meant to become stagnant. Rather, they should be temporary and task specific (Shubitz 2016).

Anytime you notice commonalities among students' work, you can teach into what you're noticing by meeting with a few students at one time. Although strategy lessons aren't as personal as one-on-one conferences, they're still highly individualized. Here are three big ways in which you might pull small groups of kids for strategy lessons:

Reteaching a
Minilesson to a
Small Group

http://sten.pub/ww26

*Missie Champagne,
fourth-grade teacher*

## On the Fly

Sometimes our teaching—no matter how carefully we plan it—doesn't reach all of our kids. You can pull a small group of students to reteach a strategy in another way. Sometimes the demonstration text may not have been right, so we use a different one. Other times, we may have gone through the steps of how to do something too quickly. Whatever the reason, anytime our teaching misses the mark, we gather that small group of students after the minilesson to reteach the minilesson in a different way.

In addition, sometimes you'll be watching what your students are doing as they work independently. You may notice students who are jumping into drafting without planning. You can pull a small group to help those kids develop strategies for brainstorming or oral rehearsal. Perhaps a few kids complain that writing is boring. Hold a strategy group to help them develop a repertoire of reasons for writing. You may discover some of your students are saying they're finished and causing their peers to lose their focus. In this case, you may want to teach these students how to add more to their drafts or how to use a peer conference when one needs help to figure out what else to write.

Finally, if you have students create plan boxes (Ayres and Shubitz 2010; also see Chapter 4, "Classroom Management") at the end of each minilesson, you might notice similar needs. Create dynamic groups based on the needs you notice when checking the way your students plan to use their independent writing time.

## After Reading Student Writing

Reading students' writing—on-demand writing, writer's notebooks, or drafts—can illuminate issues that need to be addressed. If you notice students writing personal narratives with general details, then lead a small group in which you teach students to envision what their hands, feet, and face were doing. If a few students are not using transitions in their writing, you can teach them how to use section headings or subtopics to help

them clarify their writing. Maybe several students are having trouble using ending punctuation consistently: hold a one-and-done strategy lesson about punctuating with precision. Regardless of the issue, keep sticky notes nearby as you're reading student writing so you can mark down the most pressing issue from each student's writing and then group them together with a few other peers to teach into this common need.

## Course of Study Groups

Another kind of strategy group is one that's formed intentionally with students' writing goals in mind. Writing goals are often created as an outgrowth of writing conferences or reading through students' written work (e.g., writer's notebooks, on-demand assessments, drafts). Once you've set writing goals for all students in your class, look across your students to determine which ones have similar goals. Create groups of three to five students who have the same goals. Meet with them over a period of a few weeks to teach them a course of study (Satterlee 2015) or a series of small-group lessons (Shubitz 2016) that will help them attain the writing goal they have in common.

Let's say the goal of one of the study groups is to elaborate using a variety of details. Here's what your course of study might look like:

- Session 1: Elaborate using action.
- Session 2: Elaborate using dialogue.
- Session 3: Elaborate using internal thinking.
- Session 4: Elaborate using sensory details.
- Session 5: Elaborate using setting details.
- Session 6: Final session.

Cynthia Satterlee (2015) stresses the importance of scheduling time for independent practice between each course-of-study session. After you coach your writers and they practice a strategy with you there, there is an expectation that the kids will practice the strategy you taught them during independent writing time. If you've targeted students to work on elaborating with a variety of details, you'll want to see evidence of them using their writer's notebook as a workbench to play around with that strategy and/or see instances of them writing with a variety of details in their drafts.

As you work through the course of study, it's important to see that they're continuing to use the previous sessions' strategies in their writing.

During the final course-of-study session, have each student bring their best piece of writing that illustrates using a variety of details. Each student will sit with a partner and a checklist. Ask them to do a self-assessment based on the checklist. Where did they fall? What could they do to get to the next level? You, as the teacher, don't need to be present during most of the final session since the kids are doing the work on their own. You're checking in with them and closing out the course by congratulating them on meeting their goals.

It's important to note that you may dismiss kids from the group if they've achieved the objective independently. There's no need to have a student sit through all of the sessions if you've noticed marked improvements after three sessions. In addition, courses of study can take place across different types of writing. For instance, you may start teaching students how to elaborate in narrative writing and then continue the same elaboration course of study when you begin an argument or information writing unit of study.

Finally, not all courses of study need to be six sessions, nor should they all be in one genre. For instance, if a student is having trouble elaborating with a variety of details in narrative writing, it's likely they'll have trouble elaborating with a variety of details in an informational unit of study. Therefore, courses of study can be used to transfer a skill across genres and might be as short as two or three sessions. The most important thing is to help kids master a particular skill. Any series of lessons can help students become more independent by practicing a skill repeatedly so they can master it and transfer what they've learned to any kind of writing they do.

## Assessment Groups: Using Rubrics to Score Traits of Writing

One way to make use of small groups is to involve students in the assessment process. Students can refer to a rubric for a specific trait and examine a piece of writing for strong evidence to support the use of that trait.

Let's say that students are looking for a strong focus. They can talk about the thread of a theme throughout the plot and about the breadth of the piece—too narrow, too broad, or just right. Students can discuss how the author developed her ideas. Did she use rich description, anecdotes, examples, and explanations? Did the details provide a clear picture? Did they fit the topic and make what the writer had to say believable and true? Using a rubric for the trait of ideas, students can record examples of how this text matched the criteria on the rubric and offer a score.

*Teach Writing Well* (Culham 2018) offers rubrics to score each trait in Appendix B, "Reproducible Tools." The teacher observes, listening closely to students' comments about each trait and the evidence they find in each other's pieces of writing. This structure for small group begins with an introduction of the rubric and minilessons around each trait: ideas, organization, voice, word choice, sentence fluency, and conventions. In Culham's book, consideration is also given to presentation. In the beginning, each small group may be assigned the same trait with some papers from the previous year's class with names removed. Their findings can be charted and discussed in the whole group. Eventually, the class can be divided into several small groups, and each group can examine their papers for a specific trait. Even though the students will score the papers, the purpose of this grouping is to give them a chance to deepen their understanding of the qualities of writing and be able to identify how writers use these traits to develop a piece of text.

## Interest Groups

There are myriad reasons to form small groups based on interest. Often, these interest groups are started, organized, and run by the students without much help from the teacher. Sometimes the teacher gathers information in conferences that leads to the formation of a small group of specific students to study a craft move, an author, a sentence pattern or sentence patterns, or a part of speech. Other times, students may decide to look for the power of three across the four writing types (see Shubitz 2016; Dorfman and Cappelli 2017).

## STUDYING AN AUTHOR'S CRAFT

Sometimes students are ready to extend their study of mentor texts by examining a stack of books by their favorite author. In Valerie Hawkins's fifth-grade class, the students chose a favorite mentor author to study. Mrs. Hawkins had been using mentor texts all year to help students grow as writers. Group size varied from three to six. The fifth graders gave each book in their stack a close read, placing sticky notes on pages that contained an interesting craft. Then they looked to see if they could find that same craft move in other books by the same author.

Several students formed a group to study the craft of Linda Oatman High. During their study, the fifth graders noticed that this author's word choice was so specific to each topic that even the verbs mirrored it, as in "Goosebumps sting my arms" (from *Beekeepers*), "Summertime gallops by" (from *The Girl on the High-Diving Horse*), and "My heart hammering with the sound" (from *Winter Shoes for Shadow Horse*). At the same time, the rereading of Oatman High's books led these young writers to discover hyphenated adjectives. From *The Girl on the High-Diving Horse* they found, "'That's the girl on the high-diving horse,' he explains." Another example from *The Girl on the High-Diving Horse* that shows the unique quality of these adjectives is "She's crazy-brave." From *Beekeepers*: "Grinning, Grandpa grabs his swarm-gathering tool." From *Barn Savers*: "I stack and stack, and the sun sinks low in the sky like a sleepy, red-faced farmer."

The students returned to their writer's notebook to imitate what they had discovered. Jocelyn wrote, "The lacy-fingered waves tried to overturn the kayak." She tried again: "My dad was wearing a you-should-try-this grin as he dragged the kayak onto the beach." She continued to play with hyphenated adjectives until she published her narrative "A Dream Come True" (Dorfman and Cappelli 2017). Eventually, the small groups brought their findings to the whole group, displaying their new learning on an anchor chart. They had discovered the fingerprints of their favorite authors—what those authors often relied on to build content, speak with a unique voice, and organize their writing in a logical and meaningful way.

## STUDYING A GENRE

Sometimes a small group will study a specific genre that is not introduced or does not appear in minilessons, such as graphic novels, restaurant reviews, or sports articles. Another group of students may want to study African folktales, specifically looking for the use of effective repetition in storytelling or how the author uses onomatopoeia. After studying a genre such as feature articles, a group of students may want to extend that study by examining feature articles for grammar and punctuation points and applying them to the feature articles they are creating. Using a set of feature articles from newspapers and magazines, Lynne's fourth graders focused on each author's use of questions that brought readers into the inner circle; in other words, the author asked inviting questions that seemed to address the audience in a conversational tone. The fourth graders noted that use of present-tense verbs made the piece come to life as if the events were happening before their eyes.

## STUDENT-CREATED GROUPS

Sometimes student writers take the initiative to form small groups. For example, sometimes sophisticated writers can explore several authors and the craft moves that are their fingerprints. Some students ask to form small groups based on special interests. Several students could be writing graphic novels at home even though instruction time in school has not touched on that genre. Students may request some direction for writing in this format through small-group instruction. A teacher can guide or help steer these small groups, but often, the students take charge. To challenge students, create small groups to study a genre that will not be highlighted in the whole group. Some students may work together to study and create cartoons and comic strips, restaurant reviews and travel brochures, or a science fiction piece (see Figure 8.3).

There is no end to topics for an interest group. Immersing students in a special-interest study means giving them the time to read and talk and write and talk some more about a particular topic (see Figure 8.4). These study groups can span several weeks or more. Even though students can form, plan, and share in leading small groups, the teacher observes and makes

**Ways to Structure Small Groups**

http://sten.pub/ww28

*Melanie Meehan, Elementary Writing and Social Studies Coordinator*

**Figure 8.3** Third graders decided to gather together to work on the endings to their narratives.

plans to teach by demonstration and provides support so students can practice what they have discovered in their own drafts.

## PUNCTUATION STUDY

Small-group instruction is a great way to extend conversations about grammar and punctuation. It is not about doing workbook pages or fill-in-the-blank worksheets. It is about forming new and deeper understandings of concepts and getting kids excited about language! A punctuation study is one way to help young writers appreciate punctuation and discover for themselves its purpose and effect. Students can begin by studying mentor passages with their teacher and noticing the punctuation they would like to study. From *Elsie's Bird* by Jane Yolen, fifth and sixth grade students may decide to study the uses of the commas, particularly for appositive phrases. Consider this example: "Best of all, Elsie took a little birdcage with her new canary, Timmy Tune, yellow as the sun over Boston Harbor. They sang to one another, bird and girl, along the gathering miles" (2010, 10). Once students have chosen something to study, they pore over mentor texts and books in their classroom and school library to chart examples, write a sentence or two explaining why the punctuation was necessary (what purpose it served), and then try to imitate it with their own examples.

**Figure 8.4** A kindergartner signs up for a small-group "club" to help her work on sounding out words while she's writing, which is something she's finding tricky.

During a narrative unit in Kelly Gallagher's second grade classroom, Kelly noticed that some students used effective dialogue but did not know how to use punctuation to make it easy to read. She gathered Emma, Aubrey, Madison, and Ryan to help them study their work and apply the necessary mechanics. They examined a few mentor texts, books that Kelly had already used as a read aloud such as *Elinor and Violet: The Story of Two Naughty Chickens* by Patti Beling Murphy and *Come On, Rain!* by Karen Hesse. She pulled out a favorite, *Thunder Cake* by Patricia Polacco. Kelly printed several passages onto index cards so this group could practice reading the conversations with a partner and noticing how the punctuation helped them understand who was talking and how to read with expression. Here is one of the several examples she used as exemplars to study how conversation is punctuated:

> *"I'm not brave, Grandma," I said. "I was under the bed! Remember?"*
>
> *"But you got out from under it," she answered, "and you got eggs from mean old Nellie Peckhen, you got milk from old Kick Cow, you went through the Tangled Woods to the dry shed, you climbed the trellis on the barnyard. From where I sit, only a very brave person could have done all them things!" (22)*
>
> *I thought and thought as the storm rumbled closer. She was right. I was brave! (25)*
>
> from *Thunder Cake*

Then she modeled with her own writing and asked the students to try punctuation in small steps, first deciding where to place the quotation marks. She suggested that the students try to write their conversation in play format first, using a colon after each speaker's name. She gave them several strategies to help them organize their dialogue section, including a storyboard approach with speech bubbles. Kelly wanted her students to spend their workshop time in the most effective way possible. She took the lead the first time this small group met, but when they returned several days later, they shared their progress and talked about what they had learned. Madison admitted, "The punctuation makes it easier for me to read my story. I think it is something I needed to learn how to do as a writer."

## VARIATIONS IN PRINT

Small groups can be used to help students reach a personal goal. In Shelly Keller's kindergarten class, the students were ready for something new and different. They met with Shelly to discuss possibilities for using variation in print in their journal entries. Variation in print is an exciting concept for primary students to explore since so many of the picture books they are reading make use of unusual print style. These print styles include, but are not limited to, the use of bold-face print, italics, use of all capital letters, or words in different fonts, sizes, and colors. *Muncha! Muncha! Muncha!* by Candace Fleming is a good example for primary-age students. Kolleen brought some books for them to look at—mentor texts that she had used as a read aloud such as *Mice and Beans* by Pam Muñoz Ryan, *Night Noises* by Mem Fox, and *Chameleons are Cool* by Martin Jenkins. The students noticed variation in print including size, shape, and color. They were excited to try it out in the books they were writing. Shelly inserted questions into their conversations when it was needed. The small group tried it out right there and shared their work. They had a new question: "What else can you do besides color, shape, and size?" Then they found *Roller Coaster* by Marla Frazee and decided that the letters could move across the page like an action. Although Shelly would eventually introduce variation in print to all her students, she felt that this small group was ready for a challenge. As another Kindergarten teacher, Kolleen Bell, explained, "I try to meet students wherever they are. I don't hold them back if they are ready to take a risk and try something new. We have standards to meet at each grade level, but there's room to extend the learning and go beyond the standards, I think that's important to remember."

**Figure 8.5** Kindergarten students study how authors/illustrators vary their print style so they can do it in their own writing.

## *Final Thoughts*

Small groups are an excellent place to deliver highly individualized instruction while maximizing your instructional time. Although you'll probably find yourself using small-group time to reteach minilessons, you will increase the effectiveness of your small-group instruction if you plan courses of study for your students to help them grow in specific writing skills. Remember to provide students with time for independent practice between course-of-study meetings so they will have ample time to try out the things you are teaching.

## When You're Ready

Once you've mastered pulling your own small-group sessions, you can have your students sign up for small groups based on self-identified needs. Review your conferring notes and/or student writing. Write down commonalities you're noticing. Then post a sign-up sheet for a variety of small-group lessons based on what you think your students need. Instead of offering a minilesson on this "choose your own adventure" day (Ayres and Shubitz 2010), you'll spend the minilesson time providing your class with an overview of what each small group will work on. Then, ask students to be responsible and make an appropriate choice by signing up for the small group they think they will benefit from the most. It's possible students may not choose the lesson you think they will need, but giving them the chance to determine their own path for the day is a worthwhile endeavor.

Three helpful tips:

1. Have all students make a plan—oral or written—for how they'll use their independent writing time when they aren't meeting with you.

2. All students should return to their focus spots before you begin working with the first small group. This way students are engaged with their own writing work rather than waiting around for you to meet with them.

3. Even if sign-ups go well, we suggest offering this "choose your own adventure" kind of day no more than two times per unit of study. Although it's important to give students the opportunity to have some say in what they're learning, you don't want to get too far behind with holding one-on-one conferences by offering this kind of sign-up on a weekly basis.

# Chapter 9

# Share Sessions

## Engaging All Writers to Support a Thriving Community

We know it's tempting to skip the end-of-workshop share session when students are engaged in their writing—especially on days when they're focused and working diligently. However, share sessions go beyond having kids turn to one another to read what they wrote. A great share session provides another teaching opportunity to lift the level of the whole class's writing. It also celebrates the work students did during independent writing time. All workshops should end with a share: they're a time to gather the class together in the meeting area or to highlight something while students remain in their focus spots to share and celebrate the writing they did that day. Students benefit from share sessions since they have the opportunity to see what their writing partner, another classmate, or all of their classmates did during independent writing time. Share sessions don't need to be long. They can last as little as five minutes. Having a share session at the end of every writing workshop provides closure to writers and often gives them something to think about as they ponder the work they'll do the following day (see Figure 9.1).

We've set up this chapter using the shares—content, craft, process, and progress—that Leah Mermelstein provides in *Don't Forget to Share* (2007). We also added a fifth kind of share: reflection. Although we expect you'll still do partner shares, we hope to provide you with a variety of ways to

**Figure 9.1** Partners sit knee to knee and eye to eye during an end-of-workshop share.

transform the way end-of-workshop share sessions look in your classroom.

## Process Shares

Elementary-age children are not only learning how to write well but also developing a sense of how they work best as writers. It's important for students to realize that every writer's process is a little different and no writer goes through the writing process in the same way. Therefore, it's important to shine a spotlight on students' processes so they can get an idea of how their classmates work best, which might inspire them to try something new.

- **Share something a peer has tried that you would like to try, too.** Students serve as fantastic mentors for each other. If your students are sharing their writing processes on a regular basis, you will find other students trying something their classmate has done. Most likely you'll uncover this kind of process-mimicking when you're doing research in a writing conference. When you learn that one of your students has been inspired by his peer, ask him to share what he learned from his classmate during share time. Not only will this boost the confidence of the young writer who is sharing, but it will amplify the writer whose process was inspirational.

- **Share your plans for the next workshop.** Whenever there's a lot of energy in your classroom, and there are audible groans at the end of independent writing time, you can have students think ahead to the next writing workshop. Have them plan what they'll do next. Then have a few students share with the class about where they are headed during the next writing workshop time.

- Share one thing you are going to work on as you revise your piece. We provide kids with revision strategies during minilessons, conferences, and strategy lessons. When they're in the thick of revision, it is important to get kids thinking about specific strategies they've learned that they can use to help them outgrow their original writing. If you limit students to sharing one strategy to use as they revise their writing during an end-of-workshop share, then everyone's voice can be heard.

- Share your planning strategies/graphic organizer. We provide students with different tools, graphic organizers, and strategies when we differentiate our instruction during one-on-one writing conferences. Have a student who is using a planning strategy effectively share why and how it's working with the entire class during a share session.

- Share some of your fingerprints—what you naturally do as a writer. Some kids would thrive as writers even if they didn't have our help. Have one of your natural-born writers teach their peers something they inherently know how to do during share time. Make sure, when selecting a student to do this kind of share, that they are sharing something they already knew how to do on their own that will be useful to the majority of writers in your classroom.

## Craft Shares

Revision shares in writing workshop often focus on craft, particularly the craft moves students have studied during minilessons or independently as author studies. We can highlight the craft moves our students are attempting in their writing by showcasing a variety of craft shares. Highlighting the ways children are emulating other writers helps them realize that they can write like published authors.

- Share something a peer has tried that you would like to try, too. Perhaps a student wrote in the voice of an animal, tree, or inanimate object, using a first-person stance (see books by Diane

Siebert or Molly Bang). In *Wishtree*, Katherine Applegate writes in the voice of Red, an oak tree that narrates the story. If a student wants to try this out, make sure there are plenty of mentor texts to study and imitate.

- **Share a way your craft moves help to reflect the genre of your piece.** It is important to understand the characteristics of a genre before you write in that genre. If students are writing a historical fiction piece, they will probably want to weave in references to actual historical events and descriptions of real people, even if their story is fiction. They will use invented scenes and dialogue but include authentic and believable details. A good example is *Esperanza Rising* by Pam Muñoz Ryan. If you are writing an African folktale, for example, you may use echoic words (onomatopoeia) and effective repetition. (See books such as *Why Mosquitoes Buzz in People's Ears* by Verna Aardema.)

- **Find one word from your draft that you consider to be a "gem" and share it aloud.** It works well when everyone does this and you can collect the gem words on a poster that you pass around to be displayed. Gem words are words students find valuable; they sparkle or catch the reader's eye like rubies and emeralds and diamonds. They can be words that are chosen because of their specificity such as hyphenated adjectives (*bare-branch* to describe a winter tree) or words that are unexpected such as *helicopter* (usually a noun but acting as an adjective here) to describe insects (dragonflies). A gem word could also be a new word for the student such as *voracious* to describe appetite and degree of hunger. The focus is on word choice—strong verbs, nouns, and specific adjectives.

- **Share one thing you have learned from an author you are reading that focuses on an element of craft.** There are many choices, such as the use of strong verbs and precise nouns, creating visual imagery, use of original similes and metaphors, the power of three, personification, alliteration, appeal to the senses, and developing one's voice (the piece sounds like the child—it has their stamp on it!).

- **Find the most powerful sentence you wrote today.** Invite students to think about craft by thinking about the moves they made. You might ask them, "What craft move did you use that made this sentence stand out to you?" "How did you originally write the sentence?" or "How, do you think, did the craft move improve the sentence?"

- **Complete this thought:** Have students come to the meeting area to talk or write about the kind of craft move they worked on. For instance, you can prompt them with, "As a writer I have learned . . . about [the craft move] I used in my writing today."

- **Share one place you are going to work on as you revise your piece.** Ask students, "What craft move could be helpful here?" "What mentor text(s) will you need to revisit?"

## Progress Shares

Inviting students to celebrate the progress they made during an end-of-workshop share is one of the most beautiful uses of the workshop's daily capstone time. We lift writers—especially writers who struggle—when we invite them to lead a progress share at the front of the classroom. You might find that you need to stand beside a student, particularly during the beginning of the year, during this kind of share since some kids feel uncomfortable talking about the progress they're making, especially if they're a little behind their peers. Regardless of whether a student can stand alone or needs you to do the majority of the talking, progress shares are crucial to helping kids celebrate the strides they're making as writers.

- **Talk about what you—as a teacher—have noticed during conference time.** If we're setting goals alongside students in writing workshop, then we are likely the first people to notice when a goal has been achieved. Anytime you notice a student outgrowing old goals and needing new ones during a writing conference, you can celebrate this kind of progress during a share.

- **Share a tip for a successful peer conference.** Peer conferring is hard! If you notice kids thriving during peer conferences, encourage the partnership to share what's working well with the entire class. Have those students challenge their classmates to try their tip the next time they confer with their writing partner.

- **Talk about how you wrote long.** Stamina and volume go hand in hand and seem to increase as the school year goes on. Anytime a student has increased the volume of writing he has done, encourage him to celebrate this accomplishment in front of his peers.

- **Discuss the act of deletion during revision.** One of the most challenging things we do as writers is kill our darlings. Knowing when to cut a word, a sentence, a paragraph, or even a page of writing is a skill that comes with a lot of practice (and maturity). If you have a student who has made massive deletions as part of large-scale revisions, it's important to have her talk about the progress she made as a writer by knowing when to chop out large swaths of writing in an effort to truly revise.

- **Share a risk you took in your writing.** It'll be evident during the first month of school who is willing to take risks as a writer, who would rather not, and who can't. Risk-averse students who grow into risk-takers—of any kind—should be celebrated in front of their peers. Invite students to read a part of their writing that felt risky to undertake or invite them to talk about how and why they were willing to take a risk as a writer.

## Content Shares

The quality of ideas and the development of those ideas is an important part of the writing of any piece. Within each writing type, it is important to teach students how to develop content. In informational writing, for example, their writer's toolbox could include quoting the experts, using

**Figure 9.2** In this third-grade classroom, students receive a microphone when it is their time to share their writing.

statistics, developing rich description, using anecdotes, adding examples and explanations, and offering definitions.

- **Share a way you added new content to your piece.** Invite students to use what was already in their writer's toolbox so they can talk about how they used a strategy or craft move to develop high-quality ideas. Encourage kids to support a big idea by providing details, examples, descriptions, and/or explanations as an important way to add content. Have students think of elaboration as an opportunity to pause after they say something and think to themselves, *What else can I say about this?* Building content is not about adding new ideas. It's about elaborating on ideas that are already there.

- **Share a paragraph of a piece that reflects the minilesson teaching point** (or a previous day's teaching point). For narrative writing, this may include teaching points that demonstrate how a writer plays with time (exploding a moment or shrinking a century Lane, 2015), writes descriptions of setting and character, includes splashes of dialogue, or adds content to reveal the characters to the readers (their thoughts, actions, what others say about them). For opinion writing, share details that support the main reasons and how they are developed with examples, explanations, quotes, and statistics.

- **Examine snippets from your writer's notebook.** Ask students to share one that develops content well or needs some help with content. For instance, you might ask your students, "How are you developing content in this piece?" or "How can you link this work in your notebook to a larger project you are working on?"

## Reflection Shares

There are many benefits to whole-class shares for reflection purposes. They are efficient and will benefit all your students. Whole-group reflection requires students to come prepared to talk about what they tried, what made their writing better, how they problem solved, and what they learned during a conference with another student or the teacher. To be prepared for reflection shares, students must spend time with their text, giving it a close read. This helps them understand the importance of rereading several times. Specific examples are pointed out—concerning focus, content, organization, voice, sentence fluency, word choice, and/or conventions.

It's best to write a reflection question or two on the board or another key location right after the minilesson is over, just as independent writing begins. Select a time when the whole-group reflection share of writing workshop will start after independent writing time is over and write it on the board next to or under your reflection question(s). That way, students will know to leave some time for reflection before the whole group convenes. When reflection time begins, students will gather in a designated location (often a rug near the board or chart stand, but students can remain in their seats). A discussion around responses to the reflection question(s) and other understandings that have been crystalized through the close reading of their own text will help students remember new learnings. Most of these reflection questions/statements can serve as writing-to-learn prompts across the content areas as well. Taking the time for students to discuss how they feel about their writing/learning lets them know that we value their feedback and will use it to improve our planning time, instruction, and assessment. Here are examples:

- "A question I still have is . . ."
- "I could teach . . . to others."
- "I still need some help to understand . . ."
- "Now I understand . . ."
- "I would like more help with . . ."
- "This craft move/strategy was hard to use because . . ."
- "The craft move/strategy was easy for me to use because . . ."
- "From recent minilessons, I was able to solve a problem." (Explain.)
- "Since finishing my piece, I have realized . . ."
- "Something I will try again in other writing pieces is . . ."
- "For me, the minilessons, teacher-student conference, peer conferences, use of mentor texts, student samples, whole-group discussions [include all that apply] were most helpful to reach my writing goals." (Explain your thinking.)

Whole-group reflection builds confidence and self-esteem and creates accountability for everyone. Students feel more at ease and more involved in the larger writing community. The entire class is focused and participating. Behavior problems are rarely an issue, especially if the writing community is gathered on a rug and everyone sits with his talking partner. You might wish to assign your students to a "spot" on the rug. That position, as well as a talking partner, can be changed about four times during the year. Once you know your students and their needs, you will know who might be good partners and what location is best to maximize participation and good listening behavior.

**Whole-Class Share Session**

http://sten.pub/ww29

*Catherine Gehman, fourth-grade teacher*

As students reflect on their thinking about the key question or statement placed on the board before independent writing begins, the teacher listens to them. A great deal of teaching occurs in a fairly short period of time, and everyone's a teacher—students share their insights and help someone else. The key is to let other people's thinking in, to notice and appropriate effective and creative problem-solving behavior. You have a chance to take some quick notes about possible minilessons during this reflection time. You and your students can use an anchor chart to record the use of effective strategies and craft moves, aha moments and discoveries, or the goals students set for themselves after their final reflections. You can decide what you think is most valuable as formative assessment and/or is most useful for student reference.

## Final Thoughts

Sharing our writing is one way to make reading-writing connections. When we share our writing, we get a chance to practice what being a fluent reader looks like and sounds like. Share sessions are a way to support purposeful conversations about writing and provide opportunities for accountable talk that link the work we do in writing workshop to speaking, listening, and reading. Our goal is to build and maintain a community of writers. Providing the time for students to reflect and to share writing pieces with classmates will help them build trust and respect. When students share their writing and thinking about their writing, they are sharing ideas that may move other writers in the community forward. In this safe community, students feel safe to try out new strategies, forms, and genres as well as share their personal insights. Finally, share sessions make it easier and more enjoyable to write. The goal of writing, most of the time, is to have readers who consider our ideas, learn something new, or react to our stories and poems with smiles and sometimes, tears. Teachers show student writers how much they value their writing by providing myriad opportunities to share and receive meaningful feedback. Whenever students share a sentence, a paragraph, or reflections about their writing, teachers are learning how their writers can best be supported.

# When You're Ready

It is always important to find new audiences for the students in your classroom other than you and their classmates. Here are some things you could try:

- Create share buddies with a class at another grade level. Start by pairing up once a month. If it works well, you can meet more frequently! Designate a classroom or larger area in the school to use, and pair students to share their work and offer praise and polish.

- Send a group of about five or six students every Friday to another classroom within your grade level to share their pieces. Rotate classrooms and students so that every month, all the students get one chance to read their piece (let them choose what they want to share) with another class.

- Find volunteers within the building who would be willing to listen to a piece of writing. The principal, librarian, school nurse, library and lunchroom aides, student teachers, and even the superintendent can be part of a large list of share buddies. Ask parents to volunteer to come to your classroom on a designated day to participate in writing workshop and share their writing, too, with a buddy or small group.

- Ask a student to share a problem-solving strategy or craft move that he used in his piece of writing and talk about how it worked for him and made his piece stronger. Share part of his piece with the rest of the class.

- Try the Circle Check Out, where all student authors read a line or share an update on a project or a connection with the minilesson concept (Heffernan 2018).

- Use the idea of conference clocks so your young writers can set up two or three "appointments" to gather ideas for revision. Make sure you have modeled the idea of giving a specific praise and a polish to each writer. Perhaps the most important facet of this procedure is to partner with new people every time so that new thinking can be gained from each conferring experience. You can develop good habits in your writers by using a conference clock for peer conferring. These habits include the following: creative risk taking, personal goal-setting, staying focused on tasks, using strategies to plan, organize, and revise. These young writers can challenge themselves with tasks of optimal difficulty, becoming more reflective and metacognitive, while learning about their own writing processes. Many of them will try to use the suggestions by their peers in their writing. Students practice being respectful, considerate, and specific as they share their feedback (see Chapter 7, "Conferring").

# Chapter 10

# Strategic Instruction in Grammar, Conventions, and Spelling

Grammar and conventions are often scrutinized during the final stages of a writing process and thought of as the finishing touches to a piece of writing. By the time writers are asked to consider mechanics and conventions, they are often eager to publish, celebrate, and move on to the next project. As teachers, we know the conventions of our written language are important, but we also know if we place too much emphasis on correctness, the result can be stilted writing without a voice. We need to breathe life into the teaching of grammar and conventions so our students do not see the work they do here as isolated and tedious. Many parents, school administrators, and community members place a high value on correct capitalization, spelling, grammar, and punctuation. Often, when we send writing home or post it on hallway bulletin boards, grammar, spelling, and punctuation are the only areas people critique (see Figure 10.1). Therefore, it becomes necessary to post a short letter—similar to the one Ruth Ayres (2017) shares on pages 106–107 in *Enticing Hard-to-Read Writers*—that explicitly says that the errors the children are making now aren't the same ones they'll be making a month from now, since they'll be making new errors in a month's time.

**Figure 10.1** This bulletin board display from a first-grade class's published writing also contains an anchor chart, so families can see what their children learned.

Teaching grammar and conventions is largely about editing. Students need to understand that writing going out to the public must be clearly communicated by choosing words carefully to carry their ideas and by checking grammar, usage, and conventions. Clearly communicating the intended message is the goal of every writer. We must guide students to understand how our language works. Instead of making grammar and mechanics a chore, we must engage them in learning about grammar and conventions by teaching them how to love words. Jeff Anderson and Whitney La Rocca (2017) advise teachers to increase students' understanding of how language works for both readers and writers by taking five minutes from reading workshop and five minutes from writing workshop to focus on how the conventions connect reading and writing. They talk about the power of experimentation and play to grow a love for language.

Grammar is a study of how our language is structured. When we start to understand it, we can use it to our advantage. Although read-alouds help students internalize the rhythms of words, sentences, and paragraphs (Laminack and Wadsworth 2015), we can use both explicit and implicit minilessons to explore grammar and conventions as well as study how mentor authors build sentences with parts of speech and conventions, imitating structures in our own writing when and where they apply. Dorfman and Dougherty (2014) remind us that we need to use our best judgment to determine when students need more grammar and conventions instruction to reach their target audience. It is important to remember that perfect writing cannot be taught in a year!

## Daily Oral Language

There are many reasons why daily oral language exercises do not work for students. First of all, the students are seeing sentences that have mistakes in spelling, punctuation, and grammar. Students who are highly proficient in grammar and mechanics do not need to do these exercises. The students who need the most help are seeing sentences written incorrectly, often copy the sentences incorrectly, and still do not know how to correct them. Since these isolated exercises often do not relate to our writers' immediate needs, there is no transfer even if the students can correct the mistakes. We think a culture of correctness should be emphasized. To this end, students can chart examples from their independent reading texts to understand a part of speech, such as an adverb, or punctuation, such as the apostrophe. These examples can be shared in the whole group during share time—final reflections offered at the close of writing workshop—or as part of small-group instruction. Students can search for examples in their writer's notebook or previous pieces of published writing. Holding ongoing grammar conversations with the class is a positive way to learn and to encourage experimentation.

Children's literature can be a powerful tool for exposing students to language, form, and function. Students need to ask "why" questions often. They can explore mentor texts to help them lift the quality of their

Writing Partner Conference to Help Kids Self-Manage Their Editing
http://sten.pub/ww30

*Missie Champagne, fourth-grade teacher*

writing by taking risks and trying new punctuation and sentence structures. Using mentor texts, students can read like writers and imitate the authors to shape their writing and grow as writers. We are not saying proofreading is not an important skill; we are saying proofreading activities should ask students to look more closely at their own writing, the writing where they have invested their time and their passion.

## The Sounds and Rhythms of Language

Anyone who has read "The Swing" by Robert Louis Stevenson can almost feel the back-and-forth motion of the swing that the poet has created. The cadence in this poem is created by dactylic meter, and although elementary-age students may not know the term, they can feel the rhythm. Each sentence has its own beat, and when we combine words into sentences and sentences into paragraphs, we create a kind of music. Short and long sentences give readers a chance to rush forward with breathless excitement or stop abruptly for dramatic effect. Look at the short and long sentences from this excerpt from a third grader's narrative, "Home Again." Her balance of short and long sentences helps the reader move effortlessly through her text. The three short sentences placed at the end are all Shannon needed to show just how excited her character was to see her parents after a long trip to visit grandparents in another state.

Embedding Grammar
Instruction into the
Curriculum

http://sten.pub/ww31

Stephanie Landis,
Principal

Shannon peered out the window, trying to decide if the brown smudge in the middle of snowy patches far in the distance was her city. The bright sun overhead reflected on the new January snow, making her eyes squint even as she cupped her hand over them to block out some light. Still, she could hardly see the ground. As they circled over the city and slipped down toward the landing field like a small, graceful bird, Shannon wiggled. Then she wiggled some more. As the wheels touched the ground, some of the passengers commented on a rough landing. But not Shannon. She was too busy looking out the window. As the commuter plane rolled to a stop, she pulled at her grandfather's sleeve. "Look! There's Daddy! And there's Mother, too!"

# Poetry and Song Lyrics as Mentor Texts

A great way to study the sounds and rhythms of our language is to use poetry and song lyrics. Studying mentor sentences can help students experiment with structures that create voice, tone, and music. There are powerful sentences in prose that remind us more of poetry. Can you hear the influence of *In November* (Rylant 2000) on fourth-grader Ben's reflections on the month of December? Notice how alliteration gives this piece a distinct rhythm. There is a balance in the use of two verbs and two objects of the preposition (*among*) and two actions (*sharing* and *sipping*). The repeated use of the conjunction *and* in the next sentence also provides rhythm and makes the reader feel that this list is not finite—that it goes on to include other feelings not mentioned here. The use of *In December* in the last sentence provides a bookend structure to this paragraph since the first sentence begins the same way.

> *In December, snow floats on crisp, cold air while flickering fires fill our fireplaces. We snuggle and cuddle among comfy pillows and comfy cushions to share our sledding stories and to sip foamy hot chocolate dotted with tiny, white marshmallows. We feel warm and happy and sleepy. In December, our thoughts are as free and numbered as snowflakes.*

Students may better understand how important it is to read their work aloud to develop their ear for writing by reading poetry of favorite poets and by performing their own poetry for their class and other audiences. Studying song lyrics can help them gain an appreciation for rhythms, line breaks, and the effective use of repetition to help us remember the lyrics.

# Spelling

There are many ways to help students with spelling, but memorizing lists of words and testing them every Friday is probably not one of them. Conversations about spelling can be helpful. Sometimes we can gather the writing community on the rug during our literacy block and ask them questions such as, "What do you do when you're trying to spell a tricky word?" and "How important do you think spelling is?" We may want to record some of their responses. "Do you ever have a hard time remembering how to spell a word that you used to know?" or "When you are writing, how often do you substitute another word that you know how to spell for one you are not sure of [for example, *big* instead of *colossal*]?" Since teachers often emphasize correctness in spelling, students try to compensate by writing less or choosing words they know how to spell instead of using the words they really want to use.

There are many useful spelling strategies we can teach our students. It is easy to encourage students to take a few seconds to figure out words they already know how to spell rather than write them any which way. Every Monday, spend five minutes introducing a concept. One day during the week, spend a few minutes on activities that let students explore and practice that spelling strategy, and end with a wrap-up on Friday.

Teach your students to pause when they get to a tricky word during the writing process and think, *Do I know how to spell this word?* They should think about sight words, words with familiar patterns, and words the class has studied. They can always use a strategy or the word wall or spell checker—and they should be instructed to make a good effort during the composing process to do so. Teach students to write *sp* above a word or circle it if they will need more help so they do not interrupt their process.

Teach students to use the have-a-go strategy (Snowball and Bolton 1999). Students write a word three different ways until they find one that looks right. With this great strategy, students use visual memory— make a choice—and move on with the writing of their piece. They can use the margins of the writing piece to have a go rather than go elsewhere. Other tools and resources are different-colored pens or pencils, spellcheckers, a print-rich environment, and the spelling experts in your room.

# Spelling Instructional Strategies for the Classroom Teacher

The findings that children move from concrete letter-sound matching to strategies that are increasingly pattern and meaning driven give additional weight to the practice of carefully controlling the linguistic presentation of spelling words. If spelling instruction is to meet varied developmental needs, then the use of multiple lists at the necessary development level should be a part of the ordinary instruction. Spelling instruction should use an integrated approach and needs to be a part of writing, reading, and word study. Spelling patterns should be directly taught, and spelling instruction should take into account the developmental levels of the students.

Whenever possible, invented spelling can be used to help students who are not ready for conventional spelling, regardless of their grade level. Students should be encouraged to apply what they know about sound-and-letter correspondence, spelling patterns, and rhyming words to approximate the adult spelling of a word. Invented spelling, therefore, is highly engineered, and we can learn a lot about what students know about spelling from their approximations. Differentiate instruction for all by creating a list with challenge words for some and a scaled-down list for others with the most important words that will be used in daily writing. A teacher can help students by using visualization, auditory clues, and mnemonic devices, and by presenting resources.

1. Visualization

   - Look at the word and say it aloud.
   - Picture the word and its shape (the configuration) in your head.
   - Cover the word and write it.
   - Compare your spelling of the word with the example.

2. Auditory Clues

   - Sound stretching and blending: h-a-p-p-y.
   - Use of end rhyme.

3. Kinesthetic Technique

   ◆ Trace the word in the air or in sand.

   ◆ Cut out words in sandpaper or any other textured material, and let the kids feel the letters as they say the word and spell it aloud.

4. Mnemonic Strategy

   ◆ **Dessert** has a double helping of *s*.

   ◆ **Hear** has the word **ear**. You **hear** with your **ear**.

   ◆ An **island is land** completely surrounded by water.

   ◆ Never **believe** in a **lie**.

   ◆ **Emma** faced a **dilemma**.

5. Use Resources

   ◆ Friends, teachers, parents.

   ◆ Dictionary, thesaurus, word wall, environmental print.

   ◆ Spell-check, Franklin Speller.

   ◆ Personal log (words I need to know) or spelling/vocabulary self-selection journal, individual student word banks.

   ◆ Various printed resources to identify spelling word.

   ◆ Develop strategies for finding words in text as a reference for spelling.

# Spelling Instructional Strategies for the Classroom Student

We want students to do their best with spelling in all their written work. This "Do your best!" mentality translates into spelling words correctly if we know how and trying to use highly engineered spelling (invented spelling) to get as close as possible to the conventional spelling when we are trying unknown words (see Figure 10.2).

# Spelling Strategies Self-Assessment

1. Think about what it means to be a good speller and the strategies you use to help you spell words. Some important strategies include:
   - Sound it out.
   - Ask a parent or sibling.
   - Spell the base word you know and then add the prefixes and/or suffixes.
   - Visualize the word in your mind. Where do you remember seeing it before? Think about what it looks like.

2. Use a checklist to help you remember the strategies.

3. Use a spellchecker, dictionary, thesaurus, personalized spelling dictionary, or the text where the word appears to check the spelling of a difficult or unfamiliar word.

4. Use a word you already know and change it a little (exs. Jake, make, cake).

5. Figure out how many chunks or syllables the word has.

6. Count the number of syllables and compare it to the syllables the spellchecker generates.

7. Write a word several different ways and decide which one looks right (known as have-a-go).

8. Substitute letters you know make the same sound (exs. ph/f, ck/c, c/s, g/j, ough/f).

9. Use a mnemonic device (ex. The principal is your pal.).

10. Circle or underline words or parts of words you need to check.

11. Write the word in the air.

12. Think about the shape of the word. Are there tall or short letters? Are there letters that hang below?

13. Stretch the word out and say the sounds slowly (ex. h-a-p-p-y).

14. Go to a place where the word appears such as a chart, a bulletin board, or a sign.

15. Ask for confirmation from a friend or teacher: "Is this right?"

**Figure 10.2** Students can use this tool to help them self-assess their spelling in their writing.     *(continued)*

## Spelling Strategies Self-Assessment, *cont.*

**16.** Make use of the four regular spelling rules:

- *i* before *e* rule. *i* before *e* except after *c* or when sounded like *a* as in *neighbor* and *weigh*. (exceptions: either, leisure, seize, science, society, foreign).

- Silent *e* rule: If a word ends in a silent *e*, drop the *e* before an ending that begins with a vowel. Keep the *e* when adding an ending that begins with a consonant (exs. hope + ed = hoped, care + ful= careful).

- *y* rule: Change the final *y* of a word to *i* when the last two letters of the word are a consonant + *y* or when the ending being added begins with a vowel, −*ful*, -*ly*, or −*ness*. Keep a *y* that follows a vowel or if the ending being added is −*ing* (exs. *try + ing = trying*).

- Doubling rule—Double the final the consonant of a word when:

  - The last three letters of the word are a consonant, a vowel, and a consonant (ex. fan = fanning).

  - The word is only one syllable or is accented on the last syllable (ex. begin = beginning).

  - The ending being added begins with a vowel (ex. stop + ed = stopped).

**Figure 10.2** Students can use this tool to help them self-assess their spelling in their writing, *cont.*

## Don't Save Editing for the End

When we grew up, we were taught to edit once we finished a piece of writing. As we've grown as teachers and writers, we've learned that isn't what real writers do. Rather, "[E]diting shouldn't be something writers save for the day before publication. Remind your students that writers are constantly editing. Yes, they're polishing their writing by proofreading it before taking it to publication, but editing is a daily task" (Shubitz 2017).

Editing is hard. For some, editing is painful. And perhaps editing feels cumbersome to many people because they have been taught to save it for the end. Therefore, we can teach students to do one or all of the following fixes while drafting:

- Sentence-Level Fixes: Encourage kids to reread their sentences while drafting. Do they make sense? If not, they can go back and fix their language—right then and there—to make their writing sound better.

  ◆ It's crucial to teach students how to make quick fixes so they don't become bogged down with editing while they're drafting.

- Section-Level Fixes: Some students might benefit from looking at larger chunks of their writing (e.g., when they get to the end of a paragraph or page) to search for errors and to make changes.

- Whole-Part Fixes: Fix up conventions at the end of independent writing time. That is, before coming together for the share session, encourage students to take a couple of minutes to edit their writing.

  ◆ For misspelled words: Students can circle the word and write *sp* so they can return to that word later and fix it.

  ◆ For grammar and punctuation: Encourage kids to check for age-appropriate things (e.g., capital letters and ending punctuation in the primary grades) and make quick changes.

To get kids into the habit of editing while they're writing, rather than saving it for the day before they publish, you might do one or two mid-workshop interruption or share session teaching points each week that focus on editing until the majority of your students are editing during the writing process independently.

## Strategies for Self-Editing

Unless you have access to a copyeditor, which few of us do, it's important to become your own editor. We know it's hard for adults to edit their own work, which means it's more challenging for kids to do it without introducing new errors into their writing.

Over the years, we've found a few strategies that are effective in teaching children to edit their own writing.

- **Check for Homophones** Many of the misspelled words in students' writing are homophones, which are words that sound the same but have different spellings and meanings. Serravallo (2017) suggests teaching students how to reread their sentences and put the definition of each word in its place, and then ask themselves, *Are my sentences correct?* If not, then students need to replace the misspelled word with the correct one so their sentence reads correctly.

- **Eliminate Unnecessary Words** Provide students with a short list of words they can often eliminate from their writing. (Make it a short list like the ones listed in the article you can scan on the left.) Have them read through their writing in an effort to eradicate these words from their sentences so long as the meaning remains the same. The goal is to help students economize their words by eradicating unnecessary ones that don't contribute to meaning.

- **Give Students a Lens** It's challenging for young students to identify all the errors in their writing. It helps to give students one lens (e.g., internal punctuation, punctuating dialogue, paragraphing, spelling, subject-verb agreement) to focus on at a time so they can read their work looking for just those things. Then they can go back with a different lens when they read through their text again.

- **Paragraphing** Paragraphing is more of an art than a science. Although many kids have come to us thinking a paragraph must be five sentences long, we know—as readers—that this isn't the case (see Figure 10.3). Therefore, we can teach students when to start new paragraphs (Ayres 2012; Murphy 2014).

- **Read Writing Aloud** One of the best ways to catch your own errors is to read your work—aloud, in a quiet place—exactly as it's written. If something sounds awkward, you make the change immediately. However, some students need to hear their writing read aloud *in their own ears* to help them make the necessary changes.

Here are 15 words we can teach kids to eliminate from their writing to help their writing be stronger.

- **Spelling List** Ask students to read through their writing and identify, by circling, words they think they have misspelled (Vopat 2007). From there, students can show the list to you and create a list of personal spelling words so they can learn not just how to spell these words properly on one piece of writing, but to master the spelling indefinitely.

- **To Apostrophe or Not to Apostrophe (Possessives)** One of the most common mistakes we see (even in adult writing) is the overuse of apostrophes with many words that end in s. Serravallo (2017) suggests teaching students to find words in their writing that end in s and then ask themselves, each time, whether the word needs an apostrophe (i.e., whether it belongs to someone or something). If the word doesn't show possession, students should rewrite the word without the apostrophe (if they have added it to a noun that uses s to show plural) so the word makes sense in context.

## Times to Start a New Paragraph

- A new person is speaking.
- Big idea shifts.
- Change in time.
- New place.
- New topic.
- To emphasize one word, phrase, or sentence.
- To share an anecdote or personal story.
- Tone changes.
- When the writing feels too long.

**Figure 10.3** Create a chart with your students so they understand when to begin a new paragraph.

# Who Should Be Involved in the Editing Process?

Editing is part of the writing process that is between the writer and his or her editor. In the writing workshop setting, that editor is you. Here is where your expertise comes in. The editing process should always be a discussion and instruction between teacher and student writer. It is important that students try to be their first editor in the same way that we were the first editors for *Welcome to Writing Workshop*. The expectation is that students try to write in complete sentences, use appropriate conventions, and make sure that usage is correct. Even though we love peer conferences, an editing conference is for the writer and the teacher. Peers try to be helpful, but we have found that when they offer suggestions for editing, those suggestions are not always correct. It has been our experience that students tend to trust the advice from their peers, so they sometimes take something that is correct and create an error—all based on a peer conference (Overmeyer 2015). Therefore, editing should not be part of peer conferences. Those conferences—where we look at a piece of writing that is going to be viewed by outside audiences, published in some way—should be reserved for the writer and his or her teacher. Editing is a difficult process. In the real world, we have editors who fix comma splices and dangling participles. In the classroom, we can help students with our expertise and hold them accountable to edit the things we know they can fix without our help.

# Develop a Schoolwide Plan

Many an upper-elementary teacher—Stacey included—has shaken her head and said, "I can't believe I have to teach my kids how to _____. They should have learned it before!" However, unless you have a schoolwide scope and sequence for teaching grammar and conventions, it's possible students haven't learned how to do something by the time they reach fifth grade. Too often, we assume something has been taught early on, but often, teachers don't know what kinds of grammar-related things they're responsible for teaching at their grade level.

Dan Feigelson (2008) asserts, "Once a school has begun to think deeply about the way it approaches the teaching of mechanics in general and punctuation in particular, the next step is to come to an agreement about what is expected from one year to the next" (188). Feigelson suggests creating a mechanics articulation team, which is when "one teacher representing each grade comes together with other relevant staff (e.g., literacy coaches, administration) around a particular subject area or instructional issue to come up with ideas" (188). A mechanics articulation team can meet several times to discuss what kinds of things (e.g., capitalization, commas, punctuating dialogue, sentence structure, use of tense) they expect to introduce at each grade level based on the population of the school. It is understood that mastery should be achieved the year *after* something is introduced.

Stacey and her colleagues at The Learning Community in Central Falls, Rhode Island, worked together to create a writing mechanics scope and sequence for the elementary school using the end-of-year expectations guide in Feigelson's *Practical Punctuation* (2008). After a schoolwide meeting to talk about conventions, several members of the school's staff met and tweaked the guide in Feigelson's book so that the grade-by-grade expectations worked for the large number of English language learners who attend The Learning Community.

Once your school has a schoolwide plan in place for teaching grammar, usage, and mechanics, everyone has a clearer idea of what they're responsible for introducing to students and what they should expect students to master. If students haven't mastered the previous grade's (or grades') expectations, they can be grouped together in small groups for strategy lessons to help them master whatever skills they need help mastering.

## Final Thoughts

Mechanics and conventions are ever present, tucked in during writing workshop and across the day. Sometimes, however, you will need to explicitly teach a new grammar or punctuation concept. At the beginning of the year, begin a list of grammar and editing skills you think your students need with the help of your grade-level partners. Consult Common Core State Standards or professional books by Jeff Anderson, Dan Feigelson, William Strunk and E. B. White, or Mary Ehrenworth and Vicki Vinton as well. Decide what is necessary to move the writer forward—teach the writer, not the writing!

Students will grow in sophistication as they move from grade to grade. Remember that "a growth piece" for a fifth grader does not only mean every sentence begins with a capital letter and ends with some mark of punctuation. It demonstrates that the student took some risks and tried something new—maybe using punctuation such as a colon or even a semi-colon or adding appositive and infinitive phrases. Students need to know how to be independent learners who can problem solve and figure things out on their own by consulting myriad sources. Therefore, don't just teach your writers grammar—teach them how to learn grammar!

## When You're Ready

One of the best ways to teach convention use is for students to see it in a high-quality mentor text and to be able to look for the convention in their own writing. A convention marathon is a quick way to help students move between a mentor text and their own writing. This marathon activity can be used to examine end punctuation, such as question marks and exclamation marks, or internal punctuation, such as commas, colons, and semicolons. As any experienced marathoner will tell you, you don't run a marathon every day. Therefore, use a convention marathon a few times a year, as an inquiry approach, to vary your whole-class instruction.

When using a mentor text to begin the apostrophe marathon, you can discuss how to look for any words using the apostrophe. Then, in small groups, students place sticky notes where apostrophes have been used in some way in a short section of the text (one to three pages). Once students have found the words with apostrophes, they can be categorized on a chart (singular and plural possessive and contractions). Read the sentences from the mentor text aloud, asking students to help you analyze and categorize the apostrophes used. Ask students to continue to find apostrophes in this book and other books written by the same author.

Throughout the apostrophe marathon, walk around the room, listen in, ask guiding questions, correct misconceptions, and collect information for the later whole-group reflection. Examples can be added to the anchor chart. Rich discussion about contractions and possessives will occur during this engaging experience of pulling out apostrophes from real texts, categorizing them, and finally, internalizing the patterns.

In addition, we want to provide you with a list of books that will help you and your students play with language. We think they're great references for students to take back to their writing spots to use as resources.

Bruno, Elsa Knight. 2009. *Punctuation Celebration*. New York: Henry Holt.
Features fourteen poems, each addressing a mark of punctuation and its uses.

Cleary, Brian. 1999. *A Mink, a Fink, a Skating Rink: What Is a Noun?* Minneapolis, MN: Millbrook Press.
Cleary has written a number of books celebrating parts of speech. Each book allows readers to intuit the definition from studying the illustrations.

Heller, Ruth. 1987. *A Cache of Jewels and Other Collective Nouns*. New York: Grosset and Dunlap.
Heller has many books available for demonstrating parts of speech.

High, Linda Oatman. 2003. *The Girl on the High-Diving Horse*. New York: Philomel.
This book provides opportunities to talk about the use of proper nouns and hyphenated adjectives.

Hutchins, Pat. 1968. *Rosie's Walk*. New York: Simon and Schuster.
A fox is after Rosie the hen, but Rosie doesn't know it. Filled with prepositions.

Krouse Rosenthal, Amy. *Exclamation Mark*. 2013. New York: Scholastic.
The author describes what an exclamation point does through a delightful narrative.

Loewen, Nancy. 2007. *If You Were a Conjunction*. Minneapolis, MN: Picture Window Books.

Look for other books by this author; many come with activity pages.

Martin, Bill. 1970. *The Maestro Plays*. New York: Henry Holt.

This book highlights adverbs in an entertaining narrative.

Raschka, Chris. 1993. *Yo! Yes?* New York: Orchard Books.

Punctuation matters in this illustrated narrative.

Truss, Lynne. 2006. *Eats, Shoots & Leaves: Why, Commas Really Do Make a Difference*. New York: G. P. Putnam's Sons.

Truss emphasizes comma rules in this picture book.

———. 2007. *The Girl's Like Spaghetti: Why, You Can't Manage Without Apostrophes!* New York: G. P. Putnam's Sons.

Understanding the job of apostrophes is the subject of this book.

# *Afterword*

We hope *Welcome to Writing Workshop* has helped you examine your writing classroom in new ways. It takes courage and patience to try new things and to change routines and teaching methods that make us feel safe and secure. We believe teachers must lead the way for change, helping their students wonder, be curious, develop stamina, and actively listen to members of their writing community. We want our students and our teachers to be imagineers! We envision writing workshop as a place where students and teachers engage each day in the pursuit of deeper learning fueled by their passions and purposes.

Now that you've reached the end of a journey with us, we want to remind you of something important. Please . . . have fun! We know there are standards, learning progressions, checklists, and many more things being thrown at you to show evidence of student learning. But we want you to remember the importance of creating what Ralph Fletcher calls a *writing greenbelt*. This playful, low-stakes writing brings in the joy and yields high-quality results, too. Fletcher talks about achieving a balance and advocating for things such as voice and choice in writing and valuing passion and originality. Perhaps his book *Joy Write: Cultivating High-Impact, Low Stakes Writing* (2017b) will be your next professional read. Whatever it is, we hope you will continue to read books about writing to be inspired and grow in confidence as a teacher of writers.

Academic knowledge about writing is important. Equally important is what we communicate to our students about the power of writing and how it makes us feel. When we join our student writers in the process of writing—sharing notebook entries, stories about family members, friendly letters, blog posts, poems, and more—we show them our passion and reveal who we are as human beings. We let them know we are doing what we are asking them to do. We are writing. We are writers. Together, our daily mission is to read high-quality mentor texts, to draft and revise, to get and give

**Find a Mentor**

http://sten.pub/ww32

*Stephanie Landis, Principal*

feedback, to stick with our writing when we have obstacles to overcome, to reflect on practice, and to strive to make each moment count. We want all students in writing workshop to have a writing identity—to believe they are writers at a conscious level and understand that their voice matters. As the winter and spring of 2018 showed us, young people do not have to wait until they graduate from college to use their voices to affect change.

We hope you watch our three video clips below that capture what students have to say about what they have learned in writing workshop, what new goals they've imagined for themselves to move forward as writers, and why they believe it is important to be part of a larger community of writers. They were eager to share their thinking with you.

Talking About What We've Learned in Writing Workshop

http://sten.pub/ww33

The Benefits of Belonging to a Writing Community

http://sten.pub/ww34

Goals and What We've Learned About Ourselves as Writers

http://sten.pub/ww35

Let's collaborate in the years to come. Please let us know how it's going as you implement different aspects of writing workshop. You can reach out to us on Twitter, @sshubitz and @LynneRDorfman. (Use #WelcomeWW in your tweet.)

We wish you success on your new journey and great joy!

Stacey and Lynne

*Stacey & Lynne*

# Appendices

## A List of Student Expectations

- Students will be respectful to each other and of classroom property.
- Students will use active listening skills in class discussions, conferences, and demonstrations/minilessons.
- Students will be actively engaged in meaningful writing activities during writing workshop.
- Students will be responsible for making informed decisions to revise and edit based on teacher and peer conferences.
- Students will make every attempt to write legibly, using spacing, appropriate letter formation, and punctuation.
- Students will make every attempt to approximate adult spelling by stretching out the sounds in an unknown word and blending those sounds or by consulting spell-check or a dictionary. They will use inventive spelling whenever possible so they can continue to draft instead of waiting for an adult to give the correct spelling of a word.
- Students will be able to fluently read their piece in a conference, using the picture as a guide, end punctuation, and appropriate layout features to help them.
- Students will come to conferences prepared to ask for specific help (for example, "I am having trouble including examples to support my big ideas" or "My sentences all start the same way").
- Students will refer to mentor texts and conference notes to help them revise independently before and after a conference.
- Students will demonstrate their knowledge and application of the writing process.
- Students will show evidence of their growth as a writer by trying out the new strategies/craft moves highlighted in minilessons.

*Welcome to Writing Workshop: Engaging Today's Students with a Model That Works* by Stacey Shubitz and Lynne Dorfman. Copyright © 2019. Stenhouse Publishers.

## Welcome to Writing Workshop Survey

1. What kind of writing would you like to do that you have not done yet this year?

2. Do you feel you have choice in writing topics?

3. Do you think this class feels like a community? How so?

4. Do you feel you are part of a safe and caring environment? Why or why not?

5. Do you know all your classmates, and do you invite them (or are you invited) to join writing projects and peer conferences?

6. Is there enough time to write in this classroom on a daily basis?

7. Are you happy with the pace we keep in writing workshop? Do you have any input into how fast or slowly things move?

8. Do you have opportunities to address different purposes? Different audiences?

9. What else would you like to tell me about your experience as a writer?

## Time-Savers

- Writing should be scheduled every day so that students have a sense of continuity. It is much easier to "pick up where they left off" from the day before.

- Choice, choice, choice! Students will be more willing to get started and stay engaged if they can choose their own topics and, as often as possible, their genres as well.

- Integrate test preparation into daily practice, but don't let it become the focus of what you do.

- Expect legible handwriting. You need to be able to read a piece in order to communicate feedback to the student.

- Teach basic skills in context and not in isolated worksheets.

- Expect high-frequency words and environmental print to be spelled correctly. No excuses here! This saves a lot of correction time.

- Invented spellings permit students to use a larger vocabulary. Students should circle words they think they may have misspelled.

- Make sure students have a purpose for writing. Understanding why we write is crucial for ownership and investment of energy and time.

- Make sure students write for a variety of audiences—not just the teacher! Audience awareness increases student engagement!

## Class-at-a-Glance Grid

| | | | | |
|---|---|---|---|---|
| Name:<br><br>Date:<br>Compliment:<br><br>Teaching Point: | Name:<br><br>Date:<br>Compliment:<br><br>Teaching Point: | Name:<br><br>Date:<br>Compliment:<br><br>Teaching Point: | Name:<br><br>Date:<br>Compliment:<br><br>Teaching Point: | Name:<br><br>Date:<br>Compliment:<br><br>Teaching Point: |
| Name:<br><br>Date:<br>Compliment:<br><br>Teaching Point: | Name:<br><br>Date:<br>Compliment:<br><br>Teaching Point: | Name:<br><br>Date:<br>Compliment:<br><br>Teaching Point: | Name:<br><br>Date:<br>Compliment:<br><br>Teaching Point: | Name:<br><br>Date:<br>Compliment:<br><br>Teaching Point: |
| Name:<br><br>Date:<br>Compliment:<br><br>Teaching Point: | Name:<br><br>Date:<br>Compliment:<br><br>Teaching Point: | Name:<br><br>Date:<br>Compliment:<br><br>Teaching Point: | Name:<br><br>Date:<br>Compliment:<br><br>Teaching Point: | Name:<br><br>Date:<br>Compliment:<br><br>Teaching Point: |
| Name:<br><br>Date:<br>Compliment:<br><br>Teaching Point: | Name:<br><br>Date:<br>Compliment:<br><br>Teaching Point: | Name:<br><br>Date:<br>Compliment:<br><br>Teaching Point: | Name:<br><br>Date:<br>Compliment:<br><br>Teaching Point: | Name:<br><br>Date:<br>Compliment:<br><br>Teaching Point: |

# Single Student Conference Record Form

**Name:** _____

| Date | Compliment | Teaching Point |
|---|---|---|
| | | |
| | | |
| | | |
| | | |
| | | |
| | | |
| | | |

## Single Student Conference Record Form
## with Space for Future Teaching Plans

Name: _____

| Date | Compliment | Teaching Point | Next Steps |
|------|------------|----------------|------------|
|      |            |                |            |
|      |            |                |            |
|      |            |                |            |
|      |            |                |            |
|      |            |                |            |
|      |            |                |            |
|      |            |                |            |

## Single Student Conference Record Form
## with Space for Goal-Setting and Future Teaching Plans

_____'s Writing Goals:

1.

2.

3.

| Date | Compliment | Teaching Point | Next Steps (for future conferences) |
|------|------------|----------------|-------------------------------------|
|      |            |                |                                     |
|      |            |                |                                     |
|      |            |                |                                     |
|      |            |                |                                     |
|      |            |                |                                     |
|      |            |                |                                     |

**Ms. Shubitz:** Hi there. How's it going?

**Alayna:** It's going okay. I still can't find my writer's notebook. So, I grabbed some paper and a clipboard from the writing center so I wouldn't waste time today.

**Ms. Shubitz:** That was smart thinking, Alayna. I never want you to waste a second of workshop time. I'll help you look for it before you go to lunch today.

**Alayna:** That would be nice. Thanks.

**Ms. Shubitz:** No problem. So tell me what you're working on as a writer.

**Alayna:** Well, I'm doing what you said . . . I'm taking my old timeline and redoing it.

**Ms. Shubitz:** What do you mean?

**Alayna:** I mean, I'm taking one dot from my timeline, and I'm making a new timeline just of that dot.

**Ms. Shubitz:** May I take a look at it?

**Alayna:** Sure.

**Ms. Shubitz** (*Reads Alayna's timeline.*): Can you tell me why you decided to pick this dot, about being at the dentist's office, to expand into a new timeline?

**Alayna:** Well, I think that was the most important part of my day.

**Ms. Shubitz:** Alayna, you're doing such smart work as a writer. I can tell that you're unfolding the events on your timeline bit by bit. When I looked at your timeline, I noticed you listed the events in the order in which they were happening. Right now, just from reading your timeline, I feel as though I'm right next to you, in the dentist's office. It's almost as if you made a movie in your mind about your day at the dentist's office, and you've used your timeline to retell that day with crystal-clear clarity so that even the reader of your timeline can know exactly what unfolded that day. I know this will help your reader follow the sequence

*(continued)*

of events when they read your story. Congratulations on unfolding that small moment bit by bit. Great work, Alayna.

**Alayna:** Thanks.

**Ms. Shubitz:** Another thing that good writers of personal narratives do is shift between actions and thinking. You can have some action, then some thinking, then another action, then thinking, action, thinking, and so on. What I'd like to do is show you some writing that I've been doing about the time I cut my hair for Locks of Love. I want you to notice, as I read it to you, how I start with an action, then I have some thinking, then I have more action, then some more thinking. Okay?

**Alayna:** Sure.

**Ms. Shubitz** (*Begins to read personal narrative.*)**:** So let's go back and look at what I've written so far.

**Alayna:** Okay.

**Ms. Shubitz:** It starts with my ponytail being cut off. That's action. Then I gasped when I saw that Ernesto cut off my ponytail above the rubber band, not below it. There's some thinking there since I was so upset. Do you see that?

**Alayna:** Yes.

**Ms. Shubitz:** Okay, then I run my right hand through my hair and feel how short it is. What is that?

**Alayna:** Action.

**Ms. Shubitz:** Okay, then what do I do next: action or thinking?

**Alayna:** Hold on—let me read it again.

**Ms. Shubitz:** Okay.

**Alayna:** Well, you said it was too short . . . boy short. That's you thinking about how your hair looks, so I'd say that's thinking.

**Ms. Shubitz:** You bet it is.

**Alayna:** Cool.

**Ms. Shubitz:** So now it's your turn to try it. I want you to look back at the timeline you've created. You've done a super job unfolding the events at the dentist's office in sequence. Now what I'd like you to do is add some thinking to your timeline. Since all of your actions are on the left side, why don't you write your thinking on the right side.

**Alayna:** I can do that.

**Ms. Shubitz:** Okay, I'm going to stay with you as you give it a try.

**Alayna:** (*Begins adding thinking spots on the right side of her timeline. Ms. Shubitz reads it over and realizes that Alayna understood the teaching point after she had three thinking spots that correlated with each action.*)

**Ms. Shubitz:** Alayna, I want to stop you. I noticed that you showed what you were thinking on the opposite side of the timeline each time there was an action. I want you to continue to do that for the rest of the piece after I leave.

**Alayna:** No problem.

**Ms. Shubitz:** Great. So Alayna, today and every day that you're writing a personal narrative, remember that you can shift between actions and thinking. This will help your story remain clear, but will also allow your reader to get inside your head so that he or she knows what you were thinking every time something happened to you.

**Alayna:** That makes sense. I'll try writing it with my thinking tonight.

**Ms. Shubitz:** Great. And I'll help you look for your notebook before lunchtime. Until then, if you finish your timeline, be sure to just write down your draft on a piece of paper, okay?

**Alayna:** Okay.

**Ms. Shubitz:** Great. Go ahead and get back to work.

## Spelling Strategies Self-Assessment

**Writer:** _____ **Date:** _____

Mark the strategies you use after looking through your writer's notebook and current draft. You may also use published drafts to help you respond to this self-assessment checklist.

*Put a check next to the ones you use the most.*

1. _____ I stretch words out slowly and listen to sounds.

2. _____ I draw a line under words I am not sure of during drafting.

3. _____ I clap out syllables and check each syllable for a vowel.

4. _____ I try to visualize what the word looks like.

5. _____ I use the margin or another piece of paper to spell the word several ways and choose the one that looks right.

6. _____ I use words I know to spell other words. (If I can spell *will*, then I can spell *spill*.)

7. _____ I use my "Need to Spell Correctly" or "No Excuses" list.

8. _____ I use the class word wall and all environmental print (anchor charts, bulletin board displays) to help me spell.

9. _____ I refer to the homophone lists.

10. _____ I look for patterns of spelling in my writer's notebook and published drafts to help me make good decisions.

11. _____ I use a dictionary, thesaurus, or spellchecker on the computer.

# References

Aguilar, Elena. 2017. "How to Cultivate Trust: Always Remember 5 to 1." The Coaching Teachers. September 6. http://blogs.edweek.org/teachers /coaching_teachers/2017/09/how_to_cultivate_trust_always_.html.

Anderson, Carl. 2000. *How's It Going? A Practical Guide to Conferring with Student Writers*. Portsmouth, NH: Heinemann.

———. 2005. *Assessing Writers*. Portsmouth, NH: Heinemann.

———. 2008. *Strategic Writing Conferences: Smart Conversations That Move Young Writers Forward*. Portsmouth, NH: Heinemann.

———. 2011. "Assessment-Based Writing Instruction: Use a Study of Student Work to Generate Goals and Systems for Recording Progress Towards Those Goals, K–2." Weeklong session at the Teachers College Reading and Writing Project. July Writing Institute.

———. 2018a. *A Teacher's Guide to Writing Conferences, Grades K–8*. Portsmouth, NH: Heinemann.

———. 2018b. "The Optimistic Writing Teacher." Keynote address at the Teachers College Reading and Writing Project. August Writing Institute.

Anderson, Jeff, and Whitney La Rocca. 2017. *Patterns of Power: Inviting Young Writers into the Conventions of Language, Grades 1–5*. Portland, ME: Stenhouse.

Atwell, Nancie. 1998. *In the Middle: A Lifetime of Learning About Writing, Reading, and Adolescents*. Portsmouth, NH: Heinemann.

Ayres, Ruth. 2012. "Paragraphing—Part II." *Two Writing Teachers*. September 25. https://twowritingteachers.org/2012/09/25/paragraphs-part-ii.

———. 2017. *Enticing Hard-to-Reach Writers*. Portland, ME: Stenhouse.

Ayres, Ruth, and Stacey Shubitz. 2010. *Day by Day: Refining Writing Workshop Through 180 Days of Reflective Practice*. Portland, ME: Stenhouse.

Ball, Lanny. 2017. "On the Pitfalls of Hiding Out." *Two Writing Teachers*. February 13. https://twowritingteachers.org/2017/02/13/on-the-pitfalls -of-hiding-out/.

Bishop, Rudine Sims. "Mirrors, Windows, and Sliding Glass Doors" *Perspectives: Choosing and Using Books for the Classroom.* Vo. 6, no. 3. Summer 1990.

Buckner, Aimee. 2005. *Notebook Know-How: Strategies for the Writer's Notebook.* Portland, ME: Stenhouse.

Bullock, Richard, ed. 1998. *Why Workshop? Changing Course in 7–12.* Portland, ME: Stenhouse.

Calkins, Lucy. 2012. "In the Complicated World of Today, What's Changed and What's Stayed the Same About the TCRWP's Ideas on Teaching Writing." Session at the Teachers College Reading and Writing Project Saturday Reunion, March 2012.

———. 2013. *A Guide to the Common Core Writing Workshop: Intermediate Grades.* Portsmouth, NH: Heinemann.

———. 2018. "Finding Majesty in the Comings and Goings of Our Lives." Keynote address at the Teachers College Reading and Writing Project. August Writing Institute.

Calkins, Lucy McCormick. 1994. *The Art of Teaching Writing.* New ed. Portsmouth, NH: Heinemann.

Calkins, Lucy, Kelly Hohne, and Cory Gillette. 2013. *Boxes and Bullets: Personal and Persuasive Essays.* Portsmouth, NH: Heinemann.

Calkins, Lucy, with Kelly Hohne and Audra Robb. 2015. *Writing Pathways: Performance Assessments and Learning Progressions, Grades K–8.* Portsmouth, NH: Heinemann.

Clements, Katie. 2017. "Making Literary Essays Meaningful and Beautiful." Weeklong session at Teachers College Reading and Writing Project. August Writing Institute.

Cockerille, Anna Gratz. 2014. "Table Conferences: An Important Coaching Move at the Start of the Year." *Two Writing Teachers.* August 22. https://twowritingteachers.org/2014/08/22/table-conferences-an-important-coaching-move-at-the-start-of-the-year/.

Cruz, M. Colleen. 2015. *The Unstoppable Writing Teacher: Real Strategies for the Real Classroom.* Portsmouth, NH: Heinemann.

Culham, Ruth. 2018. *Teaching Writing Well: How to Assess Writing, Invigorate Instruction, and Rethink Revision.* Portland, ME: Stenhouse.

Dorfman, Lynne R., and Diane Dougherty. 2014. *Grammar Matters: Lessons, Tips, and Conversations Using Mentor Texts, K–6.* Portland, ME: Stenhouse.

———. 2017. *A Closer Look: Learning More About Our Writers with Formative Assessment.* Portland, ME: Stenhouse.

Dorfman, Lynne R., and Rose Cappelli. 2007. *Mentor Texts: Teaching Writing Through Children's Literature, K–6.* Portland, ME: Stenhouse.

———. 2017. *Mentor Texts: Teaching Writing Through Children's Literature, K–6.* 2nd ed. Portland, ME: Stenhouse.

Dweck, Carol. 2007. *Mindset: The New Psychology of Success.* New York: Random House.

Feigelson, Dan. 2008. *Practical Punctuation: Lessons on Rule Making and Rule Breaking in Elementary Writing.* Portsmouth, NH: Heinemann.

Fletcher, Ralph. 2017a. *The Writing Teacher's Companion: Embracing Choice, Voice, Purpose, & Play.* New York: Scholastic.

———. 2017b. *Joy Write: Cultivating High-Impact, Low-Stakes Writing.* Portsmouth, NH: Heinemann.

Fletcher, Ralph, and Joann Portalupi. 2001. *Writing Workshop: The Essential Guide.* Portsmouth, NH: Heinemann.

Gladwell, Malcolm. 2011. *Outliers: The Story of Success.* New York: Back Bay Books.

Goodman, Yetta, and Gretchen Owocki. 2002. *Kidwatching: Documenting Children's Literacy Development.* Portsmouth, NH: Heinemann.

Graham, Steve, and Karen R. Harris. 2014. "Six Recommendations for Teaching Writing to Meet the Common Core." In *Write Now! Empowering Writers in Today's K–6 Classroom,* ed. Kathy Ganske. Newark, DE: International Reading Association.

Graves, Donald. 1982. *Writing: Teachers & Children at Work.* Portsmouth, NH: Heinemann.

Haskamp, Jennie. n.d. "15 Words You Need to Eliminate from Your Vocabulary to Sound Smarter." The Muse. https://www.themuse.com /advice/15-words-you-need-to-eliminate-from-your-vocabulary-to -sound-smarter.

Heffernan, Lee (@lee_heffernan). 2018. A6: Our end of workshop share session is called Circle Check Out. All authors share a line or an update on a project or a connection with the mini lesson concept. They learn from each other every day that way. https://twitter.com/lee_heffernan /status/963234744430456832.

Hertz, Christine, and Kristine Mraz. 2018. *Kids 1st from Day 1: A Teacher's Guide to Today's Classroom.* Portsmouth, NH: Heinemann.

Hesse, Karen. 1999. *Come On, Rain!* NY: Scholastic Press.

Laminack, Lester, and Reba M. Wadsworth. 2015. *Writers Are Readers: Flipping Reading Instruction into Writing Opportunities.* Portmouth, NH: Heinemann.

Lane, Barry. 2015. *After the End: Teaching and Learning Creative Revision.* Second Edition. Portsmouth, NH: Heinemann.

Mermelstein, Leah. 2007. *Don't Forget to Share: The Crucial Last Step in the Writing Workshop.* Portsmouth, NH: Heinemann.

Minor, Cornelius. 2019. *We Got This: Equity, Access, and the Quest to Be Who Our Students Need Us to Be.* Portsmouth, NH: Heinemann.

Mooney, Margaret. 1990. *Reading To, With, and By Children.* Katonah, NY: Richard C. Owen.

Moore, Beth. 2013. "Pens Versus Pencils: Which One Is Better for Writing Workshop?" *Two Writing Teachers.* November 16. https://twowritingteachers.org/2013/11/16/ pens-versus-pencils-which-one-is-better-for-writing-workshop/.

———. 2018. "Differentiating the Writer's Notebook for Every Stage K–8: Notebooks as a Writer's Tool." *Two Writing Teachers.* November 9. https:// twowritingteachers.org/2018/11/09/differentiating-the-writers -notebook-for-every-stage-k-8-notebooks-as-a-writers-tool/.

———. 2018. Resources. Retrieved from http://elizabeth-moore.com /resources-1/#/paper-choices-materials/

Murphy, Dana. 2014. "Making Paragraphing Decisions" *Two Writing Teachers*. February 5. https://twowritingteachers.org/2014/02/05/making -paragraph-decisions/.

Murray, Donald M. 1982. *Learning by Teaching: Selected Articles on Writing and Teaching*. Montclair, NJ: Boynton/Cook.

———. 2004. *A Writer Teaches Writing*. 2nd ed. Boston: Heinle.

Newkirk, Tom (@Tom_Newkirk). 2018. A great mentor text does more than show us qualities of good writing. It provokes something in us— memory, passion, a desire to write, to take our turn. https://twitter.com /Tom_Newkirk/status/971472956542017536.

Overmeyer, Mark. 2015. *Let's Talk: Managing One-on-One, Peer, and Small-Group Conferences*. Portsmouth, ME: Stenhouse.

———. 2017. KSRA Annual Conference. General Session, Hershey, PA, October 11.

Pearson, P. David, and Margaret C. Gallagher. 1983. "The Instruction of Reading Comprehension." *Contemporary Educational Psychology* 8. pp. 317–344.

Radencich, Marguerite C., Lyn J. McKay, and Jeanne R. Parratore. 1995. "Keeping Flexible Groups Flexible: Grouping Options" in *Flexible Grouping for Literacy in the Elementary Grades*. Boston: Allyn and Bacon.

Ray, Katie Wood. 1999. *Wondrous Words: Writers and Writing in the Elementary Classroom*. Urbana, IL: NCTE.

Roberts, Kate, and Maggie Beattie Roberts. 2016. *DIY Literacy: Teaching Tools for Differentiation, Rigor, and Independence*. Portsmouth, NH: Heinemann.

Routman, Regie. 2005. *Writing Essentials: Raising Expectations and Results While Simplifying Teaching*. Portsmouth, NH: Heinemann.

———. 2018. *Literacy Essentials: Engagement, Excellence, and Equity for All Learners*. Portland, ME: Stenhouse.

Satterlee, Cynthia. 2015. "Becoming More Skilled at Group Work." Session at the Teachers College Reading and Writing Project. August Writing Institute.

Serravallo, Jennifer. 2006. Teachers College Reading and Writing Project. August Writing Institute.

———. 2017. *The Writing Strategies Book: Your Everything Guide to Developing Skilled Writers.* Portsmouth, NH: Heinemann.

Shubitz, Stacey. 2007. "Keeping Track of Writing Conferences." *Two Writing Teachers.* August 19. https://twowritingteachers.org/2007/08/19/keeping-track-of-writing-conferences/.

———. 2009. *Using Mentor Texts to Differentiate for Young Writers. Statement.* 45: 24–26.

———. 2011. "Confer Like a Doctor." *Two Writing Teachers.* June 30. https://twowritingteachers.org/2011/06/30/confer-like-a-doctor/.

———. 2012. "Writing Workshop Expectations." *Two Writing Teachers.* August 23. https://twowritingteachers.org/2012/08/23/wwexpectations/.

———. 2015. "Moving from Partnerships to Peer Conferring." *Two Writing Teachers.* August 26. https://twowritingteachers.org/2015/08/26/peerconfer/.

———. 2016. *Craft Moves: Lesson Sets for Teaching Writing with Mentor Texts.* Portland, ME: Stenhouse.

———. 2017. "The Writing Process Isn't Linear. So Why Do Schools Keep Pretending It Is?" We Are Teachers. February 8. https://www.weareteachers.com/writing-process-not-linear/.

———. 2018. "End-of-Year Letters: Looking Back and Moving Forward." *Two Writing Teachers.* May 6. https://twowritingteachers.org/2018/05/06/endofyrletters/.

Snowball, Diane, and Faye Bolton. 1999. *Spelling K–8: Planning and Teaching.* Portland, ME: Stenhouse.

Tolan, Kathleen. 2015. "'Once You Have Taught Workshops for Years, How Do You Go from Good to Great?' Tap the Power of Peer Conferring and Supporting Student Independence and Goal-Setting." Session at the Teachers College Reading and Writing Project. August Writing Institute.

Tomlinson, Carol A. 2001. *How to Differentiate Instruction in Mixed-Ability Classrooms.* Alexandria, VA: Association for Supervision and Curriculum Development.

Upper Grade Summer Institute Writing Packet. 2005. Teachers College Reading and Writing Project.

Vopat, Jim. 2007. *Micro Lessons in Writing*. Portsmouth, NH: Heinemann.

Vygotsky, Lev. 1986. *Thought and Language*. Rev. ed. Cambridge, MA: MIT Press.

## Children's Literature Cited

Aardema, Verna. 1992. *Why Mosquitoes Buzz in People's Ears*. New York: Scholastic.

Applegate, Katherine. 2017. *Wishtree*. New York: Macmillan Publishers.

Fleming, Candace. 2002. *Muncha! Muncha! Muncha!* New York: Atheneum Books for Young Readers.

Fox, Mem. 1992. *Night Noises*. New York: HMH Books for Young Readers.

Frazee, Marla. 2008. *Roller Coaster*. New York: HMH Books.

Hanlon, Amy. *Ralph Tells a Story*. 2012. New York: Two Lions.

Hesse, Karen. 1999. *Come On, Rain!* New York: Scholastic Press.

High, Linda Oatman. 1998. *Beekeepers*. Honesdale, PA: Boyds Mills Press.

———. 2001. *Winter Shoes for Willie*. Honesdale, PA: Boyds Mills Press.

———. 2003. *The Girl on the High-Diving Horse*. New York: Philomel Books.

———. 2012. *Barn Savers*. Honesdale, PA: Boyds Mills Press.

Jenkins, Martin. 2001. *Chameleons Are Cool*. Somerville, MA: Candlewick.

Murphy, Patti Beling. 2001. *Elinor and Violet: The Story of Two Naughty Chickens*. New York: Little, Brown.

Polacco, Patricia. 1997. *Thunder Cake*. New York: Puffin Books.

Raschka, Chris. 2011. *A Ball for Daisy*. New York: Schwartz and Wade Books.

Ryan, Pam Muñoz. 2002. *Esperanza Rising*. New York: Scholastic.

Ryan, Pam Muñoz. 2001. *Mice and Beans*. New York: Scholastic.

Rylant, Cynthia. 2000. *In November*. New York: HMH Books.

Yolen, Jane. 2010. *Elsie's Bird*. New York: Penguin books.

# Index